Contents

0188800

Resources in Edu... ...ore the last date shown below.

School Development Planning

A Practical Guide to the Strategic
Management Process

Corrie Giles

Northcote House

Resources in Education

Other titles in this Series:

Adventure in Education, Richard Andrews (in preparation)
Beyond the Core Curriculum, Mike Harrison (Editor)
Developing the Child with Down's Syndrome, Joyce Mepsted
  (in preparation)
Evaluating the Primary School, Brian Hardie
Local Management of Schools, Brent Davies & Chris Braund
Managing the Primary School Budget, Brent Davies & Linda Ellison
Managing Stress in Schools, Marie Brown & Sue Ralph
Teaching Science in the Primary School, Alan Cross & Gill Peet (Editors)
  Book 1: Source material; **Book 2:** Action plans (in preparation)
The Language of Discipline (2nd edition), Bill Rogers
Reading Voices: Children talking about the books they read, Fiona Collins,
  Phillippa Hunt & Jacquie Nunn (in preparation)
The School Library, Elizabeth King
The School Meals Service, Nan Berger
Time Management for Teachers, Marie Brown & Sue Ralph
  (in preparation)

ISBN 0 7463 0626 1

British Library Cataloguing-in-Publication Data
A catalogue record for this book is available
from the British Library

First published in 1997 by Northcote House Publishers Ltd,
Plymbridge House, Estover Road, Plymouth PL6 7PY,
United Kingdom.
Tel: Plymouth (01752) 202368. Fax: (01752) 202330.

Typeset by Kestrel Data, Exeter
Printed and bound in Great Britain

Preface

This book has been written to provide a clear and straightforward guide to school development planning in the light of experience gained during the difficult transitional years immediately following the 1988 Education Reform Act. Rather than attempting to produce an academic text on the subject, I have provided an approach to development planning that is understandable and usable in our rapidly changing primary and secondary schools.

The book is designed to improve the strategic management of the various stages of the planning *process*, as well as to provide clear guidance on how to produce effective working documents. It avoids jargon and is written with the needs of busy professionals or interested lay-people very much in mind.

The book should be of equal value to LEA officers, headteachers, governors and teachers who are seeking to clarify their role in the school planning process, or who wish to explore the potential of planning for sustaining an effective approach to managing quality through whole-school *improvement* and *development*.

As the school development plan (SDP) is the starting point for *monitoring* and *evaluating* school performance, this book should also be useful reading for governors, senior staff and teachers anxious to review their earlier development plans in advance of the four-yearly cycle of inspection by the Office for Standards in Education (OFSTED). It should also provide useful reading for newly qualified OFSTED inspectors, as well as for management consultants working with schools on pre-inspection reviews.

This, then, is the essential purpose of the chapters that follow: to provide a comprehensive user-friendly guide to site-based planning for a wide range of people who are professionally involved in the education service, and who are seeking a management tool for **co-ordinating, supporting** and **sustaining** the process of change.

Chapter 1 provides a brief overview of the emergence of development planning in LEAs and schools in recent years. A number of issues are raised in relation to OFSTED and school inspection, which will help schools to review their existing development plans and, perhaps, question the focus and construction of their existing documents in a changing planning context.

Chapter 2 takes a more formal look at the nature of plans and clarifies the difference between strategic plans, school development plans and action plans. The chapter identifies a number of misconceptions and confusions concerning the hierarchy of school plans that need to be closely co-ordinated for site-based planning to be really successful.

Chapter 3 is concerned with the process of planning, in particular whole-school planning as a collaborative activity. The stages in the whole-school planning process are identified and explored, as are the additional benefits to schools of a well managed planning process.

Chapter 4 is the key chapter of the book and concentrates on **managing the process** of producing a school development plan. The chapter explores the key stages of strategic review, auditing progress and ensuring action, and provides a framework which schools will find useful for producing their own SDP documents.

Chapter 5 looks at the benefits, as well as some of the problems, of implementing a school development plan. A number of practical solutions are provided to the problems experienced in a case study school, where the SDP approach to site-based planning has yet to prove entirely successful.

Chapter 6 provides detailed examples of school plans, including the structure and outline content of a strategic plan, a school development plan and an action plan. Useful management tips are provided to help avoid some of the more common pitfalls.

Chapter 7 suggests an approach for evaluating both a school development plan and the school planning process, using, in part, OFSTED documents. The chapter contains a questionnaire and check lists which will be invaluable to any school as part of its pre-inspection review.

Chapter 8 concludes the book and summarises the key issues for improving school planning in general and school development planning in particular. A number of other suggestions are also included. These concern probable planning trends in the future and link strategic planning and school development planning to likely changes in the funding of education, and the management of quality and accountability.

Those readers who wish for a more academic look at school development planning will be able to refer in more detail to the works of a variety of authors which appear in a short bibliography at the end of this book.

Acknowledgements

I am grateful to my former colleagues and postgraduate students at the Crewe and Alsager Faculty of Manchester Metropolitan University with whom I have shared and developed so many of the thoughts contained in this book.

I would also like to thank Brian Hardie for stimulating my initial interest in planning and his subsequent support and encouragement; Roland Seymour for his editorial assistance and wisdom; my former teaching colleagues throughout Cheshire LEA for sharing their experience and, last but not least, my wife Sue Collins for her tireless support and endless proofreading, but most of all for her love.

1
The Changing Planning Context

Between 1988 and 1993 three major Education Acts were passed in England and Wales which have radically altered the planning context for Local Education Authorities (LEAs) and schools. The combined effect of this legislation has been to establish a market economy in the education service which is intended to increase **efficiency**, improve the **quality** of teaching and learning, and promote the **accountability** and **responsiveness** of a much more diverse state school system, through increased **competition** and greater **parental choice**.

The main vehicle for implementing government policy was the introduction in the 1988 Education Reform Act of the Local Management of Schools (LMS) initiative, which has fundamentally altered the traditional planning relationship between central government, LEAs and schools. By delegating resources and the responsibility for decision-making to schools, responsibility for planning improvement and development was effectively transferred away from LEAs, and their power and role reduced to the provision of:

- information and advice;
- monitoring, evaluating and reporting progress in schools;
- inspection and support;
- certain services which were centrally retained in the interests of efficiency;
- training and development via locally administered central government grants.

Unfortunately, the transition from LEA to school site-based

1

planning varied considerably as traditional relationships adjusted to the realities of the new legislation. The legacy of this transitional period is worth exploring briefly, as the effects of some of the earlier approaches to site-based planning are still influencing the quality of the planning process which has developed in some schools.

The purpose of this chapter is, therefore, fourfold:

- to review briefly the changes that have occurred in the national, LEA and school planning context in recent years;
- to suggest some of the planning issues likely to be facing schools in the future;
- to identify the causes of some of the initial problems encountered by LEAs and schools adjusting to their new planning responsibilities;
- to raise a number of issues which will assist schools in reviewing their existing development plans and in questioning the direction, focus and purpose of their existing planning approach.

THE EVOLUTION OF SITE-BASED PLANNING

Although the strategic importance of site-based planning was recognised and encouraged at the outset of the LMS initiative, schools were not entirely free to plan the use of their delegated resources. The Department of Education and Science (DES), in their official guidance for the introduction of LMS schemes in England and Wales (Circular 7/88), envisaged a continuing, albeit temporary, strategic planning role for LEAs. Five key factors variously influenced LEAs to embrace SDPs as their preferred approach to site-based planning during the LMS transition period:

- the need to collect a wide range of information as evidence for the DES that centrally imposed reform was being effectively implemented;
- the need to develop a means of monitoring progress in their schools, and provide support and advice in implementing the new legislation;
- the need to respond to central government controls imposed by legislation, statutory orders and 'earmarked' development grants which required specific plans from schools, including

a **staff development plan**, a **financial management plan** and a **National Curriculum development plan**;

- the residual power retained by LEAs to insist that their schools had an SDP, and which allowed some LEAs to retain a surprising degree of control over the form, focus and purpose of site-based planning in their schools;
- the considerable professional interest in the SDP approach to site-based planning promoted by the DES-funded School Development Plans Project (DES, 1989; DES, 1991) and supported at that time in some of the key UK literature on school improvement.

THE BENEFITS OF SCHOOL DEVELOPMENT PLANS

The literature produced by the DES, LEAs and academics in support of the SDP approach to site-based planning typically portrayed SDPs as a means of helping schools to manage change. In particular, it was considered that the SDP was a useful means of bringing together the medium-term planning priorities of the school and that, although reflecting national, LEA and school policies, it could also be used to identify and implement a limited number of whole-school improvements and developments. At their best SDPs were seen as flexible working documents which provide clear *evidence* that a coherent planning process exists in a school, and that:

- the long-term *strategic* aims and goals of the school are linked to medium-term planning priorities identified in the SDP, and in turn to short-term project action plans concerned with implementation;
- *tactical* priorities are systematically identified in the SDP and resourced as part of a planning cycle which links strategic planning and the budgetary process to *operational* plans concerned with implementation;
- operational action plans support implementation of the SDP by specifying targets, identifying success criteria, establishing time lines for completing tasks and naming the people responsible for carrying them out. They also provide a framework for monitoring, evaluating, controlling and reporting on progress.

In addition, an effective SDP process was also seen as a means of encouraging:

- a collegiate and participatory approach to school planning;
- a sense of ownership amongst the staff for the specific planning responsibilities allocated to them in the SDP;
- the development of a school planning cycle which provides a coherent framework within which to make decisions;
- a clear link between staff development needs emerging from the school appraisal process, and the needs of the school identified in the SDP.

A MANAGEABLE APPROACH TO PLANNING?

These are impressive claims and surprisingly few authors have challenged the appropriateness of the SDP approach in a school system relatively inexperienced in whole-school planning. Prior to the 1988 Education Reform Act, schools had mainly *administered* the planning policies of the LEA, or engaged in the short-term planning of specific initiatives, rather than *managed* system-wide change in an uncertain legislative environment. Experience of managing whole-school change was, therefore, comparatively rare and professional working practices had evolved accordingly. Change, when it did take place in schools, was usually small scale, incremental and required a limited professional response.

Certainly a manageable approach to planning, implementing and sustaining change was needed in LEAs and schools. After all, the cumulative impact of government legislation has produced a relentless catalogue of new developments. However, such was the frequency and ambiguity of some of the government legislation that many schools seemed only able to *react to*, rather than *plan for*, the changes pressed upon them. Progress in the strategic planning of change in schools seems to have been slowed by four factors:

- a tendency to see the individual changes imposed by central government as somehow unconnected and, therefore, not to recognise the strategic direction of government thinking and *policy*;

- a difficulty in accepting the importance of planning ahead because of repeated changes to the National Curriculum, ill-thought-out schemes of assessment at the various Key Stages, and other well publicised uncertainties, as the workable *detail* of government policy became established;
- too much change and uncertainty making it difficult for senior management to be confident in planning the strategic direction of their schools;
- the challenge of establishing support for whole-school planning approaches amongst teachers, when the details of government policy seemed to change so frequently.

Although standard LEA proformas were often provided to assist schools with their first SDP, they tended to be a *multi-purpose* method of collecting information for central government and furthering the aims of the LEA, rather than a well-thought-out means of supporting site-based planning.

With proformas often arriving in school late in the academic year and out of sequence with the school's planning cycle, there was little opportunity for senior staff to consult with governors and teaching staff, or to question the *relevance, purpose, focus and timing* of the SDP approach adopted by their LEA. The proformas tended to be completed with a minimum of effort 'to keep the LEA happy'. As a result, 'first edition' SDPs varied enormously in quality, as did their usefulness as a focus for managing change and systematically planning for school improvement and development.

Unfortunately, the initial lack of emphasis placed by *some* LEAs on the importance of establishing an effective site-based planning process seems to have adversely influenced attitudes in schools, even though the LMS initiative is now well established.

AN UNDERCURRENT OF CONCERN

Sufficient time has now elapsed since the introduction of the LMS initiative for there to be growing concern at the lack of systematic planning taking place in what is now a relatively experienced, decentralised school system. There has been considerable progress in some schools and LEAs in adopting a more professional approach to site-based planning in recent years, but a survey of 106 schools by Giles (1995a) confirms that there is still cause for concern at the lack of coherent planning (see Chapter 7, page 108). Although this cannot be generalised to the school population as a whole, in about half of the schools surveyed:

- planning seemed ad hoc, with little whole-school strategic planning taking place;
- there appeared to be little *conscious* link between long- term strategic aims and goals, and the use of resources to improve and develop the school systematically;
- the SDP seemed isolated from the strategic plan, as well as from action plans concerned with implementation;
- in about two thirds of the schools surveyed, action plans were not complete enough to control implementation. As a result, the SDP was seen, in effect, as a list of 'jobs to do', rather than an agreed set of medium-term priorities which were being systematically resourced and implemented;
- monitoring and evaluating progress towards implementing policy priorities was noticeably lacking.

THE IMPACT OF OFSTED

Significantly, OFSTED, created by the 1992 Education Act to inspect schools on a four-yearly cycle, has begun to insist upon a more systematic approach to site-based planning as part of the OFSTED inspection process. Final OFSTED reports will now include:

'A judgement on the quality of the school development plan, its usefulness as an instrument for change and development, its realism and the achievement of any priorities set.'

(OFSTED, 1992)

It is possible to identify six areas from *The Handbook for the Inspection of Schools* (HMSO, 1992) which clarify what OFSTED expect to see in terms of site-based planning:

1. Information and documents
In addition to a wide range of policy documents, each school will have to produce a prospectus containing the aims and goals of the school. They will also have to produce an SDP that:

- reflects the aims, policies and goals of the school, and contains clear, costed priorities;
- indicates staff development issues for the school and individual members of staff, and addresses how these are to be met;
- includes subject or curriculum plans to demonstrate that the requirements of the National Curriculum are being systematically implemented and resourced.

As part of a **systematic review process**, a school could ask itself a number of key questions:

- are all these documents available?
- do the documents meet with the information requirements of the inspection process?
- do the documents provide evidence according to the criteria outlined in the inspection handbook?

2. The parents' meeting

Schools are required as part of the inspection process to arrange a meeting between parents and the registered inspector. This is an important meeting, as the interaction between parents and the registered inspector will be a more informed debate if **parental participation** in the life of the school has been well managed. Some of the key questions to ask in a review would be:

- have the parents been involved in the strategic planning process setting the future direction of the school?
- can they articulate a vision of the school's future?
- have parents contributed to the aims and goals of the school?
- do they know and accept the aims and goals as appropriate for their children?
- have the short-, medium- and long-term plans of the school been communicated to, and accepted by, the parent body?
- did the parents contribute to the SDP? Does the school see the SDP as part of the communication process with parents?
- is the registered inspector likely to hear well informed opinion, or hearsay, myth and gossip about the school?
- could the same questions be answered positively by the staff and governors?

3. The efficiency of the school

OFSTED intend to use the SDP as the starting point for evaluating the efficiency of the school. Their evaluation crieteria to be used make it clear that:

'An efficient school . . . analyses its use of resources in the light of priorities identified in the school development plan.'

(OFSTED)

However, in an inefficient school:

'The deployment of available resources is not closely related to educational priorities named in the school development plan.'

(OFSTED)

The inspection report will also include:

'An evaluation of . . . the efficiency with which expenditure is managed and the effectiveness with which funding is deployed to implement the goals identified in the school development plan.'

(OFSTED)

These issues raise a number of questions for schools as they review their approach to site-based planning:

- is there a systematic resource allocation process that matches resources to the priorities identified in the school development plan, or is resource allocation somewhat ad hoc and incremental?
- are our aims and goals linked by the budgetary process to the priorities identified in the school development plan, or are they separate documents/processes?

4. Planning and management

In evaluating evidence of effective planning in a school, OFSTED will judge:

'the extent to which the school has a means of evaluating its provision, identifying strengths and weaknesses and maintaining a development plan to address priorities. Plans are assessed in terms of whether the priorities for action are appropriate; whether the implications of the development programme have been assessed (including an assessment of the costs, steps to be taken, staff to be involved and training needed); and whether criteria have been developed to evaluate success.'

(OFSTED)

This quote is a very useful indication that OFSTED will be looking for evidence that the SDP is a working document that reflects an active evaluation process and is linked to action planning. Schools might wish to ask themselves if their SDP is a 'live' working document which is part of an approach to delivering quality improvements and developments in the school.

In terms of school management, the inspectors will be looking at **management processes** in the school, in particular the procedures by which decisions are made and communicated. OFSTED will also evaluate the effectiveness of:

'planning procedures and meetings, on the success of staff in meeting development targets and on the effectiveness with which senior staff facilitate change and development through appropriate organisation and deployment of resources. An evaluation of the effectiveness of the school's own review procedures'.

(OFSTED)

OFSTED will also consider an important aspect of the planning process, namely how closely practice in the school reflects the policies stated in various planning documents. They give an interesting example in the OFSTED handbook which refers specifically to SDPs:

'When read in sequence, for example, to trace the formulation of the school development plan through successive meetings, the documentation can provide clear evidence of the successive stages in policy-making, the success of consultation with parents and staff, the frequency with which issues raised result in action, and how far the priorities in the school development plan have influenced planning and spending'.

Again this quotation raises a number of questions for the school:

- does practice follow policy, or do planning documents

represent laudable aims that are rarely implemented in practice?
- is it possible to trace a clear planning process through various planning documents?
- does the school consult and facilitate participation, or are plans the product of a limited constituency?

5. Curriculum planning

In terms of subject or curriculum planning OFSTED will wish to see subject or whole-school curriculum plans, and receive evidence as to how curriculum planning is reflected in the priorities identified in the school development plan. This asks schools to consider whether curriculum planning has been co-ordinated across the school, with priorities brought together under the umbrella of the SDP.

6. Action planning

Action planning is seen by OFSTED as a vital part of the SDP in actually implementing the priorities for change that have been identified by the school. However, action points will also be produced for each school in the final inspection report, and these will have to be drawn together in an action plan by the governing body.

The procedure to be followed by the governors is laid out in DFE Circular 7/93, paragraphs 42-4, although the following notes are based very closely on a brief pamphlet, *Understanding School Action Plans*, issued jointly by OFSTED and the DFE in 1994. Details of the procedures to be followed are given in full, to underline how seriously planning is being treated by OFSTED as a means of improving schools.

ACTION PLANS AND SCHOOL INSPECTION

Every school must prepare an action plan within 40 working days of receiving its inspection report from the Registered Inspector. The law normally places responsibility for the plan upon the governing body. The governing body should:

- consult the staff in drawing up the plan;
- set out in the plan the steps the governors intend to take to tackle the issues identified in the report.

For each key issue identified in the inspection report, the action plan should:

- quote the issue from the report and outline the tasks which need to be completed to tackle it;
- state clearly and in detail what action will be taken;
- ensure that the proposals can be achieved and can be monitored;
- set a deadline for the action. Some will be short-term targets, eg within three months, some medium-term, eg within 18 months and others longer-term, eg 18 months or more;
- state the resources needed. It is necessary to consider carefully whether existing resources could be used more effectively or redeployed, or whether new resources are needed;
- name the person(s) responsible for making sure that the prescribed action is taken;
- identify who will be asked to help with the action from within and outside the school;
- state how progress in tackling the issues will be monitored, who has responsibility for the monitoring, to whom and in what form they should report.

One person or a small group should be responsible for overseeing the implementation and progress of the plan.

The length of the action plan will depend on the number of issues which require attention, but the plan must contain enough detail to allow governors, and external monitors such as HMI, to see what has been achieved and what else needs to be done.

It may also be necessary to revise the SDP in the light of the action points in the inspection report, to ensure that both are following similar lines, although action points responding to the inspection report should be clearly identified.

After completing the action plan, the governing body must send it within five days to:

- the parents of all the pupils registered at the school;
- everyone who is employed at the school;
- OFSTED;
- the LEA, or for a Grant Maintained School (GMS) the Secretary of State;

- the people who appoint the foundation governors (if any);
- the local Training and Enterprise Council (TEC), if a secondary school.

Copies must also be made available to any member of the public, and a single copy provided free to anyone living within three miles of the school. Parents may, if they wish, make a response to the action plan, either individually, through parent/governor representatives, or at the annual governors/parents meeting. Progress made in implementing the action plan should be covered in the annual report to parents.

Since action plans in themselves are the end product of the planning process, schools will have very little time to implement a full planning cycle in response to the action points identified in the final inspection report. As a result, schools will need to ask a number of questions about their ability to respond to an inspection report **before they are inspected**:

- is our existing planning process capable of responding so quickly?
- are vital stages in our planning process missing or deficient? Is there for example a strategic plan containing the aims and goals of the school? Do we have action plans which systematically implement the SDP?

A GLIMPSE OF THE FUTURE?

The emphasis on school development planning in the various guidance sections of *The Handbook for the Inspection of Schools* seems to have encouraged schools to look once again at their approach to planning as part of their pre-inspection review process. Certainly the trend for schools to consider introducing a more professional approach to planning is a timely development in such a rapidly changing management context (see Chapter 8). The government's commitment to a philosophy of competition and choice as a means of improving efficiency and quality has recently been underlined in the 1992 White Paper *Choice and Diversity*, and the 1993 Education Act. Although it is beyond the scope of this book to explore the significance of recent legislation in detail, one quote from *Choice and Diversity* summarises the government's vision of education in the twenty-first century and underlines the importance of schools developing a more sophisticated approach to site-based planning in the face of the challenges yet to come:

> 'If children are to receive the best education possible, it is a pre-requisite that they attend school and recognise their responsibilities – to others as well as themselves. Once there, they deserve the best education possible. That, as we have seen, depends upon decisions made locally – ensuring the efficient use of resources and concentration on particular educational needs – and on strong leadership. High standards will be fostered through testing, specialisation, rigorous inspection and ever-deepening recognition of the needs of individual pupils.'

Within these very clear policy parameters, locally managed schools will have to *individually* plan the development of their particular niche in the educational marketplace, identify the type of school that they intend to become, and develop a range of services for their various intended client groups. This will require schools to undertake a more searching review of the role of site-based planning than that currently being undertaken in response to OFSTED. It will also require a wider appreciation of the significance of strategic planning, development planning and action planning in improving schools and providing quality services.

However, there is a danger that, as was the case with LEAs at the start of the LMS initiative, schools will once again allow the spectre of *operational* accountability to an external agency to divert their energies away from the need to develop a strategic management approach to site-based planning.

2
Planning Revisited

Chapter 1 explored the changing planning context now facing schools; the history and impact of the SDP approach to site-based planning favoured by LEAs, and OFSTED's growing concern at the lack of planning emerging from their inspection of some schools.

The purpose of this chapter is to provide the basis for a better understanding of the nature, purposes and potential of planning. This is not as straightforward as it may seem, as management textbooks are often full of oversimplified definitions of what constitutes a plan, and what is involved in the process of planning. As a result, there is a surprisingly common tendency to confuse certain types of plan, or to miss out completely key stages of the planning process such as strategic planning. The effect of these common misunderstandings can be seen in the construction of some of the standard proformas used by LEAs, and the actual development plans produced by individual schools.

For school development plans to be successful, they need to have emerged from a systematic planning process. The planning process *integrates* the various levels of planning that exist in the school, and ensures a logical progression from *policy formulation* to *policy implementation* within the planning hierarchy.

It is important that schools are clear about the hierarchy of plans which they need to produce from their planning process. This will help them to initiate a more professional approach to site-based planning than presently reflected in 'first edition' school plans, or in many of the plans being hurriedly revised in preparation for OFSTED.

WHAT IS A PLAN?

There are many different types of plan in a school, each with a very specific purpose, and therefore, very different *style* and *content*. The style and content of the plan should reflect and support the purpose of the plan, and the level of use for which it is intended in the school. Put another way, there should be considerable differences between the style and content of the curriculum plans prepared by an *individual* classroom teacher; plans needed to ensure the safety of a *group* of children engaged in an outdoor activity; or plans intended to support the implementation of a *whole-school* curriculum initiative.

The need to distinguish between purpose and level of use is not always recognised in the planning culture of schools. All too often, planning is disjointed and incremental, with the same bureaucratic management approaches being used to produce any plan in the school, regardless of its purpose or level of intended use. As a result, much planning activity is regarded by teachers as top down, with planning decisions imposed from above. There is often very little opportunity for staff to participate in, and feel ownership of, the plans which they are supposed to be implementing.

Despite the sometimes overwhelming need for a school to change, inappropriate management approaches, which ignore the importance of creating a positive attitude towards planning, can induce a reluctance amongst the staff to adopt a more rigorous whole-school approach to the planning process. Lack of ownership, in particular, can also lead teachers or particular interest groups to focus upon their personal *operational* needs, or the needs of their particular area of responsibility, rather than establishing a planning process concerned with whole-school improvement and development. In such negative circumstances, plans tend to be vague (but often elaborate!) promises of action some time in the future, rather than operational plans which state very clearly the decisions that have been agreed, and which are then actually *implemented*!

TYPES OF PLAN

It is possible to identify the need for two broad types of plan in schools. These are known as **strategic plans** and **operational plans**.

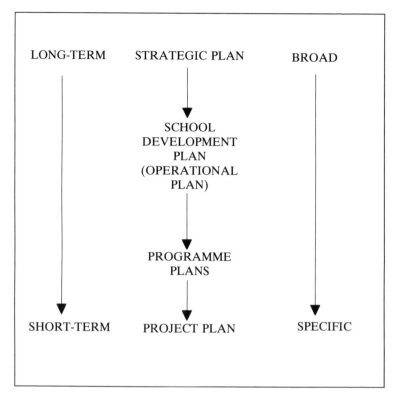

Figure 2.1 A Hierachy of School Plans

For clarity these two broad types of plan may be subdivided into various parts as shown in Figure 2.1. This figure shows the hierarchy of plans that will exist in a school with a well developed rational planning structure, and may be used as a model for evaluating the extent to which planning in a particular school has progressed so far.

It is worth spending some time looking at the two broad types of plan in more detail, as a lack of awareness of the various types of plan, and their subdivisions, can lead schools into trying to implement too many planning decisions at the same time. This in turn leads to unsurmountable problems of co-ordination and control, as teachers discover that they simply do not have the time nor a background in whole-school planning to follow elaborate procedures laid down by senior management.

WHAT ARE STRATEGIC PLANS?

A strategic plan *communicates* decisions that have been agreed concerning the *long-term* (usually five-year) development of the school. The strategic plan will reflect the values, vision, mission, aims and policies of the school, and these will shape and guide the planning goals for the future.

Establishing the right goals for the long-term development and wellbeing of a school, within the constraints of limited resources, takes up a considerable amount of planning time and is a significant challenge for the governors and senior staff.

MANAGEMENT TIP 2.1 The Missing Link
Strategic plans are frequently missing in schools and should not be confused with the brief list of aims and goals commonly found in the statutory school prospectus and often replicated at the beginning of the SDP. Neither should schools assume that because they have a mission statement and have produced their policy documents for OFSTED, these in any way form part of a strategic plan, *unless* the mission statement and policy documents have emerged from a coherent strategic planning process.

WHAT DOES A STRATEGIC PLAN CONTAIN?

Although a strategic plan is *broad* in nature, it provides a **guiding framework** for agreeing the priorities for improvement and development in the school. Priorities are implemented by the various programme and project plans which make up the medium-term (normally three-year) operational plan (SDP) of the school. The strategic plan contains:

- a statement of the **mission** of the school which clearly and succinctly provides the purpose and focus for all planning;
- the long-term **aims** which the school intends to pursue in working towards achieving its mission;
- an indication of the **broad policies** adopted by the school, which in turn will determine a list of **mandatory** and

discretionary goals which the school will prioritise and then attempt to implement.

Some textbooks suggest that, since the priority goals of the school will reflect internal and external conditions, the strategic plan should also contain a large amount of contextual and audit information, including:

- details of the planning structure of the school, including brief descriptions of the decision-making machinery; the planning responsibilities of particular significant individuals and groups, and their level of involvement in the planning process;
- a brief socio-economic outline of the planning context of the school at the time of writing;
- a 'current position statement', containing a brief audit of the key activity areas of the school, highlighting emerging trends and their influence upon present and future planning priorities.

In practice, adopting such a suggestion would make the strategic plan rather cumbersome. The approach used in Chapter 6 suggests that schools should establish a **planning handbook**, in which only the introduction contains contextual and audit information. This allows both the strategic plan and the SDP to be brief **working documents**, which are more likely to be used by busy teachers!

WHAT ARE SCHOOL DEVELOPMENT PLANS?

As the **medium- to short-term** operational plan of the school, the SDP is much more specific in nature than the strategic plan. The SDP emerges from a **tactical** planning process (see Chapter 3) which:

- prioritises a limited number of the goals from the strategic plan;
- evaluates and costs alternative approaches for using the scarce resources of the school to achieve its goals, and then
- agrees a number of single-use plans which are concerned with implementing the priorities selected (for specific examples see Chapter 6).

MANAGEMENT TIP 2.2 A Plan Too Far!
It is crucial to limit the number of priority goals selected for implementation. Otherwise there is a real danger that the school will submerge under so many layers of planning that nothing will be achieved. Chapters 4 and 5 provide a number of suggestions on how *not* to manage this stage of the planning process.

WHAT ARE SINGLE-USE PLANS?

Single-use plans are intended to bring about specific *non-routine* changes relating to the goals of the school and are dissolved when these changes have been accomplished. Single-use plans may be divided into two broad groups – **programme plans** and **project plans**.

PROGRAMME PLANS

Programme plans are the essence of the school development plan. They act as an 'umbrella' which brings together a number of **interconnected projects** concerned with implementing the **mandatory** and **discretionary goals** of the school. At the time of writing, programmes would exist to implement the following mandatory goals:

- the various Key Stages of the National Curriculum;
- National Curriculum testing, recording and reporting of pupil attainment;
- records of achievement, and
- a staff appraisal programme.

Discretionary programmes would be concerned with implementing improvements and developments based upon information obtained from internal audits and external market research. At the present time, it is likely that discretionary programmes would be limited by the amount of mandatory planning that is currently required.

PROJECT PLANS

Project plans are the smaller and separate portions of programmes. The project plan is not free-standing, it resides within
the 'umbrella' of a specific programme plan, and is concerned
with implementing one particular mandatory or discretionary
goal. Individual projects have limited scope and would, therefore,
be much more manageable in terms of implementation.

An example of a project plan would be the introduction of
Key Stage Two primary science as one aspect of the school's
mandatory National Curriculum implementation programme. In
this particular example it would become the responsibility of a
designated team or individual to implement the Key Stage Two
science project plan.

The main problem in implementing a large number of programme and project plans is the difficulty of managing several
concurrent programmes, each with its own timescale for implementation, and each supported by a variety of interconnected
projects widely distributed throughout the school. Unfortunately,
the complexity of managing the implementation of concurrent
programme plans can defeat the most able manager, particularly
when the details of government policy keep changing. Once again,
the danger is that the programme plan within which individual
projects reside is poorly managed, and that the various project
plans forming part of that particular programme are patchily
implemented or, worse still, not implemented at all. However, a
well thought out SDP supported by a well managed development
planning process can prove to be an invaluable tool for mitigating
and, to some considerable extent, overcoming such problems.

One practical way of overcoming these difficulties is to link
both programme and project plans to a particular planning
technique called **action planning**.

ACTION PLANNING

Action planning is not a *type* of planning, it is a planning *technique*
which has already been introduced in Chapter 1. The technique
is not restricted to programme or project plans, but may be used
throughout the school with other types of plan. However, the
technique is most valuable at that point where decisions have
been made about *what* should happen and been put into a plan,

but then have to be translated into action. **Action planning** takes the programme or project plan several stages further by **assigning responsibility** for action. In fact, action plans are very much the control mechanism through which the SDP can be implemented. For example, a typical action plan would show:

- the major **targets** which need to be achieved to implement a particular goal;
- the **resources** allocated and their intended purpose;
- the group or individual responsible for each **task** in the process;
- a **task time line** giving the order and timing of each task in the action plan and
- **success criteria** (agreed in advance at the planning stage) for monitoring and evaluating progress.

To return to our earlier example, in a science project action plan, a named person – a science co-ordinator – would be responsible for the five major steps given above. Task responsibility would be clearly designated, resources allocated, task time lines tied in and, most significantly, action expected. Progress would be monitored by a designated line manager at specified intervals and success evaluated against predetermined criteria built into the project plan at the outset, *not* bolted on as an afterthought once the project has been implemented.

CONCLUSION

There are, therefore, two broad types of plan, each with a very specific purpose and level of use in a school. The strategic plan will be broad in style as well as content, and have a long-term time frame. It will communicate decisions in writing concerning the agreed mission and goals of the school, and provide a framework or reference point to guide action. It is the template against which all other planning activity takes place.

The operational plan (SDP) will be more specific, although the priority goals that it is working towards will be clearly stated in the strategic plan. The SDP is concerned with a medium- to short-term time frame, and its essential purpose is to maintain progress with the existing successes of the school, and also bring about improvement and development through programme plans and project plans linked to the action planning technique. Figure 2.1 summarises these ideas as a model which represents the strategic plan, SDP, programme plans and project plans as a connected hierarchy which needs to be managed into place in any school.

Effective planners recognise this hierarchy and are careful not to confuse strategic planning with school development planning. Neither do they attempt to use the action planning technique in isolation, without having first established a well managed whole-school planning process concerned with producing and implementing whole-school strategic and operational plans. They acknowledge that the real secret in producing, implementing and sustaining successful plans is not in the production of pieces of paper, but in the *quality* of the planning process that has taken place beforehand. After all, it could be argued that the simplest part of the planning process from instigation to implementation is the writing of the actual plans. Yet some approaches to managing the planning process seem to be more successful at achieving success than others, and this, the successful management of an effective planning process, will be the focus of Chapter 3.

MANAGEMENT ISSUES 2.1

A number of questions are included here which are intended to promote discussion, and which may help to clarify some of the management issues which emerge as schools review their plans:

1. Is there a connected hierarchy of plans in the school, or are plans simply an ad hoc collection?
2. Is the school clear about the relationship between SDPs and other types of plan?
3. Does the style and content of plans in the school reflect the purpose for which they are intended?
4. Does the school lean towards incremental planning (bit by bit reactions!) or is the operational plan (SDP) clearly linked to a well developed strategic plan, and supported by a coherent whole-school planning approach?
5. Do the plans of the school support action, or are they statements of what the school would like to do in an ideal world some time in the future?

3
The Planning Process

Planning as an intentional process is not easy in periods of great change and uncertainty, nor in an environment as complex and busy as a school. Even the best laid plans can be disrupted, when there appears to be little time to do anything other than *react* to the latest legislation, statutory order, or political fashion.

Whole-school planning offers a way forward through the maze that faces schools in the wake of so much recent reform and, as an approach, it is very much concerned with *moving towards* a more rational response to managing change. Whole-school planning is supported by the philosophy:

- that it is better to draw up a rational plan to determine in advance what should be accomplished and how it should be done, rather than to react constantly to change;
- that rational planning should minimise time wasting, and avoid damaging the morale and motivation of teachers by using an *incremental* approach to planning;
- that rational planning is recognised as a complex, *on-going*, multi-level activity, not a single annual event.

However, making whole-school planning work as an approach to managing change requires the support of a well designed, clearly understood, and *actively managed* planning process.

The purpose of this chapter is to examine in general terms the working of a successful whole-school planning process as a prerequisite for successfully implementing school plans. This will entail:

- clarifying the **nature** and function of whole-school planning;

- considering the **benefits** of whole-school planning for managing school improvement and development;
- identifying the **stages** in the whole-school planning process;
- outlining some of the **strategies** for successful implementation.

WHAT IS THE NATURE AND FUNCTION OF WHOLE-SCHOOL PLANNING?

Whole-school planning is essentially a process for producing plans which are working documents and which determine in advance what should be accomplished in the school over a variety of time scales. More importantly, the process integrates the two types of plan discussed in some detail in Chapter 2:

- the strategic plan and
- the school development plan.

The whole-school planning process has five key functions:

- **maintaining** the quality of current levels of performance;
- **improving** performance where there is cause for concern;
- **developing** new initiatives which enhance the overall quality of teaching and learning in the school;
- acting as a means of **co-ordinating** an orderly transition from current to future levels of performance;
- focusing management efforts on the use of the planning process as a strategy for **recognising, implementing** and **sustaining** the changes that are required in the school.

OTHER FUNCTIONS OF THE PLANNING PROCESS

However, there are many additional advantages to a school from a well managed planning process. Firstly, whole-school planning can improve decision-making in the school by providing a systematic approach to problem solving which focuses upon:

- defining problems;
- analysing problems;
- developing alternative solutions;
- choosing from alternatives and
- making decisions effective.

Secondly, whole-school planning is not only concerned with deciding what should happen and how it should happen, it also focuses on the implementation of change by using the actual planning process as a control mechanism which ensures that change does indeed happen.

Thirdly, whole-school planning provides a useful means of facilitating the professional development and growth of those participating at the various levels in the process, by:

- improving confidence, competence and capability;
- building trust in the ability of the management team to handle change;
- minimising frustration, anxiety and, therefore, stress;
- optimising the use of staff time;
- empowering people and
- enabling leadership.

THE WHOLE-SCHOOL PLANNING PROCESS

There are four stages or **levels** involved in whole-school planning:

- The **normative planning** stage – concerned with *identifying* corporate values, vision, aspirations and mission;
- The **strategic planning** stage – concerned with *agreeing* corporate aims, goals, and policies which reflect a 'vision of the future as it should be' (Handy, 1985);
- The **tactical planning** stage – concerned with *gathering* information, evaluating alternatives, establishing priorities, taking decisions over the allocation of resources and establishing responsibilities for achieving the goals identified in the current SDP;
- The **operational planning** stage – concerned with *implementing* the priorities communicated in the SDP by means of programme and project action plans.

It is worth considering these four key stages in more detail.

NORMATIVE PLANNING—WHERE DO WE WANT TO BE?

This is the first stage in the process of producing a successful strategic plan for the school and it is concerned with identifying 'where the school wants to be' in terms of its development in the future. It is often ignored as the starting point in the process, and yet is the basis of effective whole-school planning. Normative planning consists of a series of deliberately managed whole-school planning events at which the long-term vision and aspirations of the school are agreed as a school mission statement by the various participants in the process. Normative planning requires that senior managers create the time and enthusiasm in the school for an exploration of educational values and beliefs as the basis of future planning needs and is concerned with such key questions as:

* why do we exist as a school?
* who are we here to serve as a school?
* what services are we trying to provide within the limitations of our resources?
* where will we 'position' ourselves in the emerging educational marketplace in the years to come (see Chapter 8)?

The normative stage of planning underlines the importance of a school having an overall philosophy of what it is trying to achieve and where it is going in the rapidly changing world of the future. Herein lies the danger. Great caution is needed in implementing this stage of the whole-school planning process, if busy teachers are not to 'switch off' from what can appear to be a somewhat esoteric approach to planning before they reach the pragmatic 'doing stage' (see Management Tip 3.1).

DETERMINING STRATEGY – WHERE ARE WE NOW?

Having agreed collective values and aspirations, the next stage of the planning process involves producing a 'position statement' – an honest evaluation of where the school is now – in terms of its stage of development. The statement provides the basis for determining which of the school's long-term goals need to be

---

MANAGEMENT TIP 3.1 Getting Started

Fullan (1992) cautions against too systematic an approach to planning at the *beginning* of the change process. Too much time spent in agreeing values, sharing a vision of the future and writing a mission statement can stall real progress. He suggests a four-stage cyclical approach of:

- READY – senior managers should be committed to the change, be well prepared and understand that change is a process, not an event;
- STEADY – change should not be rushed and time is needed to agree a vision of the future, establish an appropriate climate, and learn to work collegially so that real improvement is possible;
- FIRE – get going with a limited number of teacher-focused changes that give some real success and make people want more of the same;
- AIM – success provides the opportunity to implement a more professional planning cycle—agree a mission for the school; base change on data gathered in a systematic assessment of progress; plan change focusing on the characteristics of effective schools; stress agreement and ownership for successful implementation and finally evaluate success to continue the cycle.

---

emphasised as the planning agenda in future plans. However, teachers are pragmatic and it is important, if future plans are to be implemented successfully, to focus upon achievable goals emerging from the position statement, rather than the somewhat esoteric 'educational aims' commonly found at the front of school prospectuses.

Halton Board of Education (Ontario, Canada) suggest that goal-orientated school planning will be more effective with teachers if the process focuses upon the three core characteristics of what is now known by researchers to make schools more effective (see Management Tip 3.2). The Halton model has been incorporated in the planning examples to be found in Chapter 6 (See Stoll and Fink, 1992).

MANAGEMENT TIP 3.2 Ensuring a Focus

In addition to planning to implement national and local policies, school planning should also act as a vehicle for systematic whole-school improvement and development. This can be achieved by emphasising planning goals which focus on the characteristics of effective schools. These characteristics may be grouped as:

A COMMON MISSION
- shared values and beliefs;
- clear goals;
- instructional (curriculum) leadership.

AN EMPHASIS ON LEARNING
- frequent monitoring of student behaviours;
- high expectations;
- teacher collegiality and development;
- instructional and curriculum focus.

A CLIMATE CONDUCIVE TO LEARNING
- student involvement and responsibility;
- physical environment;
- recognition and incentives;
- positive student behaviour;
- parental and community involvement and support.

DETERMINING TACTICS – HOW ARE WE GOING TO GET THERE?

This is the stage of the whole-school planning process where a number of achievable goals are adopted from the strategic plan, and prioritised in the SDP for implementation in the medium term (up to three years). Various tactics can then be evaluated to determine 'how we are going to get there', before finalising how the limited resources at the school's disposal are to be used to achieve the priorities in the SDP. Again, the approach used with teachers will influence whether the SDP is perceived in the school as a practical and workable document, worthy of the meeting time that has been spent on it.

DETERMINING OPERATIONS—MANAGING THE JOURNEY

Once alternative tactics have been considered and firm policy goals identified for implementation, operational planning—'managing the journey' – takes over. This is the action planning stage where short-term programme and project plans are implemented by staff who have committed themselves to the development priorities of the school through:

- their involvement in the four key stages of the planning process;
- the support and control of implementation provided by the action planning technique;
- their individual commitments made during the school appraisal process, which is linked to the implementation of the SDP.

The combination of personal commitment and the action planning technique should ensure that the right plans are implemented at the right time, by the right people, with minimum effort and maximum efficiency. The key management principle at this crucial operational stage of the planning process should be 'management only by exception', ie there should be no need, other than on an exceptional basis, for senior management team (SMT) involvement at this stage. This in turn 'frees off' more SMT time for strategic planning and strategic management.

DESIGNING AND IMPLEMENTING THE PLANNING PROCESS

If such an approach to school planning is to prove a successful management technique for implementing and supporting change, schools may wish, first of all, to review the design of their existing planning mechanisms and supporting infrastructure. As part of this review, the school could work through the specific steps of the model summarised in Figure 3.1 and check for any weaknesses or omissions in their approach.

Although models are popular for clarifying the stages in any process, a common weakness in schools is to interpret the planning model in such a way that the process becomes too bureaucratic. This makes it very difficult to integrate and co-ordinate the implementation of the various plans that exist in the school and ensures that the planning system is slow to change. Care must be taken to think through a planning approach that is user-friendly (fit for purpose) at all levels in the school. In

1. REVIEW THE SCHOOL STRATEGIC PLAN
2. AGREE LONG-TERM AIMS AND POLICIES
3. AUDIT THE PRESENT POSITION OF THE SCHOOL
4. COLLECT INFORMATION FOR DECISION-MAKING
5. IDENTIFY MEDIUM-TERM GOALS
6. EVALUATE ALTERNATIVE STRATEGIES FOR THE USE OF RESOURCES
7. AGREE PRIORITY PROGRAMMES
8. PRODUCE A DRAFT SCHOOL DEVELOPMENT PLAN
9. CONSULT BEFORE AGREEING THE FINAL SDP
10. GAIN BUDGETARY APPROVAL AND ALLOCATE RESOURCES
11. FORMULATE PROGRAMME AND PROJECT ACTION PLANS
12. SET PERFORMANCE TARGETS
13. ASSIGN RESPONSIBILITIES
14. AGREE TASK TIME LINES
15. MONITOR PERFORMANCE
16. EVALUATE PERFORMANCE AGAINST TARGETS
17. FEEDBACK AND REVIEW

Figure 3.1 Steps in the Whole-School Planning Process

deciding fitness for purpose a number of management issues will need to be reviewed, and openly and honestly discussed (see Figure 3.2).

---

1. Has an integrated whole-school planning process been developed and what *evidence* is there that this process is working?
2. Has the whole-school planning process produced a strategic plan to guide all other planning in the school?
3. Is there genuine strategic, operational and action planning in the school, or is planning really incremental and ad hoc?
4. Is the school aware of the additional benefits of the whole-school planning process?
5. Are the governors, senior staff and teachers experienced in whole-school planning?
6. How successful has the school been in the past at managing into place and *sustaining* whole-school initiatives?
7. What is the existing culture towards planning in the school?
8. Do the governors and senior management lean towards top down, or collegiate approaches to site-based planning?
9. Do the structures and responsibilities in the school support a whole-school or an incremental planning approach?
10. Is there to be consultation with, and/or participation of various stakeholders in the planning process?
11. If there is to be participation in the planning process, what is an appropriate level of involvement for governors, SMT, staff, parents and pupils?
12. Does the school have in place a system to evaluate the quality of the planning process?
13. What, if any, are the training needs emerging from the planning review?

Figure 3.2 The Whole-School Planning Process—Key Management Issues

The answers to these questions will reveal a great deal about the existing planning culture of the school, and may suggest that a different management style is needed. If, for example, the planning process in the school is usually autocratic, hierarchical and 'top down', a move towards more openness and 'bottom up' participation in the decision-making process would need to be gradually implemented.

If, however, participation is commonplace because of existing flat management structures, care would need to be taken that a very structured and systematic whole-school planning approach is not interpreted as the introduction of an authoritatian management style. This is particularly so at the action planning stage when the talking has to stop, and some action actually take place!

Even if great care is taken at the start of the review process, there will still be a number of obstacles to overcome, and these are considered in more detail, along with a number of practical solutions, in Chapter 5.

CONCLUSION

To manage maintenance, improvement, transition and development by means of the whole-school planning process will never be easy for the management of any school. However, whole-school planning can provide enormous benefits for senior staff, by:

- increasing awareness of the school's vision and mission;
- encouraging collegiate/participative management styles which lead towards implementation of change rather than the documentation of desired change;
- improving whole-school identity;
- providing planning approaches which enable change to be implemented in a rational manner with predetermined goals, rather than through the more typical incremental, reactive and somewhat political approaches;
- identifying future opportunities and problems while there is still time to do something about them.

It should not always be assumed that those involved in planning share an understanding that the whole-school planning process has a number of purposes in addition to that of producing plans!

It is therefore important to pay particular attention to *how* whole-school planning is introduced, so that the approach actually facilitates and sustains change in a school.

Whatever approach is selected, it must be appropriate for that particular school, and designed into the process before planning is attempted. This will require 'high order' management skills and the support of a well designed, clearly understood and actively managed process. In management terms, this establishes the 'rules of the game' and the level of involvement of the 'players' *before* the planning 'game' begins.

4
Producing a School Development Plan

Schools were not obliged to produce an SDP until OFSTED began to require them under the terms of the 1992 Education Act, although individual LEAs could make SDPs compulsory in their own schools. Consequently, 'first edition' SDPs varied considerably in terms of their quality and usefulness as an approach to site-based planning (see Chapter 1). Typical examples contained the broad aims and goals of the school; a summary of the school timetable or curriculum return; a few brief notes concerning National Curriculum implementation and some indication of staff development needs. New developments were usually presented as lists of 'jobs to do', sitting somewhat uncomfortably within the brief subheadings of a standard LEA proforma. In general, 'first edition' SDPs tended to lack a clear sense of strategic direction, were focused predominantly on the curriculum and were essentially summaries or descriptions of what was happening or, hopefully, about to happen in a school.

With SDPs now a mandatory requirement for OFSTED, schools are once again looking at their plans and planning process to check that they comply with the expectations of the four-yearly cycle of inspection. The 1993 Education Act also makes considerable demands on the **strategic planning capabilities** of schools now that they may choose to apply to change their character, specialise in terms of curriculum and select pupils by ability (see Chapter 8).

Both of these developments underline the need, in some cases, to revise existing approaches to development planning and adopt a more strategic approach concerned with whole-school improvement and development. Therefore, the purpose of this chapter is to:

- clarify the nature of school development plans;
- establish an outline structure for a development plan;
- suggest what a school development plan should contain;
- identify the stages in managing the production of a successful school development plan.

WHAT IS A SCHOOL DEVELOPMENT PLAN?

A school development plan is the medium-term operational plan of the school. It emerges from the whole-school planning process discussed in Chapter 3 and is the link between the long-term strategic plan and a number of short-term programme and project action plans.

WHAT IS A SCHOOL DEVELOPMENT PLAN FOR?

A school development plan is intended to be a flexible working document which is *reviewed at least annually* and is therefore responsive to changing circumstances. It brings together in one plan the school's priorities for change and, although reflecting national, LEA and school policies, is primarily concerned with identifying and successfully implementing a limited number of whole-school improvements and developments.

THE BENEFITS OF A SCHOOL DEVELOPMENT PLAN

School development planning can be most beneficial when governors, staff and other stakeholders are involved in a continuous cycle of planning activity which:

- establishes a sense of direction for the future activities of the school as a whole;
- identifies and co-ordinates the agenda for change;
- reduces the quality gap between objectives and performance by sequencing priorities for action;
- broadens the planning of improvement and development **beyond a sole concern with curriculum planning**;

- facilitates the careful allocation of scarce resources to specific targets for improvement and development;
- identifies roles, responsibilities and success criteria against which performance may be evaluated;
- enables a more effective response to unexpected events.

In essence a development plan helps a school to:

'organise what it is already doing and what it needs to do in a more purposeful and coherent way. By co-ordinating aspects which are otherwise separate, the school acquires a shared sense of direction and is able to control and manage the tasks of development and change.' DES (1989)

WHAT DOES A SCHOOL DEVELOPMENT PLAN CONTAIN?

There is no prescribed structure to a school development plan, and advice seems to vary considerably as to what it should look like. As a result, it can be difficult to strike a balance between a simplistic proforma that reads like a list of 'jobs to do', and an over-elaborate booklet which may impress, but can hardly be said to be functional.

Although the content of development plans is also, *in theory*, freely determined by each individual school, in reality recent legislation, educational trends and parental expectations dictate much of it. Typically they will contain:

- **prescriptions** – what **must** be done in the school, and is therefore unavoidable, such as the staged implementation of the National Curriculum;
- **expectations** – what **should** be done in the school, such as improving teaching and learning styles or creating a non-sexist, non-racist school environment;
- **predilections** – what the school **would like to** do, such as broadening pupil's horizons and expectations.

However, an increasing number of prescriptions are beginning to emerge from DES/DFE or OFSTED documents concerning the content of SDPs. For example, DES Circular 12/91 expects that:

'Appraisal should be set in the context of the objectives of the school which will generally be expressed in a school development plan. Appraisal should support development planning and vice versa.'

More recently, the OFSTED *Framework for the Inspection of Schools* (1992) included a number of specific references to the content of SDPs. Some of these expectations are outlined in Figure 4.1 and others are discussed in more detail in Chapters 1 and 7. As a result of these accumulating limitations, a structure for compiling an SDP is suggested in Figure 4.5. Within this framework, individual schools will need to decide the content of their individual SDP and carefully balance external expectations with their own internal goals for improvement and development.

- the SDP should reflect the aims, goals and policies of the school and have clear, costed priorities;
- the SDP should contain subject or curriculum plans that demonstrate that the requirements of the National Curriculum are being systematically resourced and implemented;
- the SDP should give a clear indication of staff development issues for both the school and individual members of staff and how these are to be met.

Figure 4.1 The SDP and OFSTED Inspection Requirements

PRODUCING A SUCCESSFUL DEVELOPMENT PLAN

Determining the content of the SDP and producing a realistic working document will require senior management to design and implement a carefully thought through planning process (see Chapter 3 and the case study in Chapter 5). The process will need to be:

- **selective** – taking into account the school's size, context, staff strengths and present stage of development;

- **systematic** – consisting of a three-phase planning cycle which involves review, auditing progress and ensuring action;
- **focused** – only dealing with two or three major priority programmes;
- **ongoing** – projecting activities for maintenance, improvement and development over a significant period of time;
- **communicative** – informing a variety of interest groups about the planning activities of the school;
- **comprehensive** – including projects which relate to staff interests and concerns, as well as those responding to national, LEA and school improvement initiatives.

The key element in the process of producing the SDP is the systematic management of the three phases of the **school planning cycle**:

- REVIEW;
- AUDITING PROGRESS;
- ENSURING ACTION.

In practice, the three phases of the planning cycle can be broken down into a number of logical steps (see Figure 4.2, but also refer back to Figure 3.1, page 30 in Chapter 3) and these are discussed in some detail to conclude this chapter.

Phase One: Review

Step One – Conduct a management review
The first step of the management review requires the SMT to evaluate the quality of the planning process in the school as a whole. It is important for the SMT to remember that it is not always the managed that erect barriers to change. Stoner (1982) points out that managers often have an 'internal resistance to establishing goals and making plans to achieve them'. There is also the pressure created by managers themselves:

- the overwhelming pressure exerted by managers for short-term results; the urgent always receives more attention than the important. The tyranny of the urgent!

- the tendency for managers to look for short- to medium-term results, rather than developing a longer-term view;
- the problem of convincing managers that the time spent on planning is worth all the effort amidst the pressures of the here and now;
- the poor quality of information upon which managers base their decisions.

The SMT may wish to consider Chapters 2, 3 and 7 as a basis for their initial discussions. Figure 4.2 can also be used to check that all the steps in the existing approach used by the school are in place and appear to be operating effectively.

STEP 1 – CONDUCT A MANAGEMENT REVIEW

STEP 2 – REVIEW THE SCHOOL PLANNING CONTEXT

STEP 3 – REVIEW THE SCHOOL PLANNING TEAM

STEP 4 – REVIEW THE PLANNING CYCLE

STEP 5 – AUDIT THE PRESENT POSITION

STEP 6 – IDENTIFY MEDIUM-TERM PROGRAMME PRIORITIES

STEP 7 – EVALUATE ALTERNATIVE RESOURCE STRATEGIES

STEP 8 – PRODUCE THE DRAFT SCHOOL DEVELOPMENT PLAN

STEP 9 – CONSULT BEFORE AGREEING THE FINAL SDP

STEP 10 – GAIN BUDGETARY APPROVAL AND ALLOCATE RESOURCES

STEP 11 – IMPLEMENT PROGRAMME AND PROJECT ACTION PLANS

Figure 4.2 Managing the Steps of Producing an SDP

Step Two – Review the school planning context

The second step of the management review involves looking carefully at the planning context in which the school has to operate. The SMT needs to identify any changes in circumstances which are likely to influence the quality of the planning process during the next planning cycle. These include:

- the **time scale for implementing the plan – one year is rarely enough;**
- the **size** of the school;
- the **resources available** to facilitate change and development;
- the **skills available** amongst the governors, senior management and staff in whole-school planning;
- the **micropolitics** of the school;
- the quality of existing **control mechanisms** to ensure that plans are actually implemented;
- the **opportunity cost** of using so much time on planning when there are competing alternatives for management and staff time;
- **attitudes** towards planning that are prevalent in the existing culture of the school.

These factors will be considered in more detail in Chapter 5.

Step Three – Review the school planning team

Step three of the strategic review requires the SMT to consider how well the existing school planning team (SPT) has performed and to select, if necessary, a new team of people to manage the development planning process. The team could consist of the SMT, or a representative group which could include governors, senior management, teachers, support staff and pupils. Whatever approach is adopted the SMT will need to:

- clarify the role and level of involvement of the various stakeholders;
- be in overall charge of co-ordinating, monitoring and evaluating progress.

The planning team, in particular, should be given the explicit brief to gather planning information, prepare draft project proposals and, where necessary, present alternative courses of action to the

SMT. The SPT would normally have an *advisory* rather than executive function.

Step Four – Review the school planning cycle

Once the level of involvement in, and responsibility for, the planning process in the school has been established, the planning team will need to review the timing of the key steps in the whole-school planning cycle. The timing of the cycle should be determined in advance to:

● ensure coherence of the planning process,
● provide a focus for gathering information and preparing decision-making briefs for various school committees and
● co-ordinate appropriate involvement of the various stake-holders.

Although a typical whole-school planning cycle would normally be five years, in times of great change and uncertainty it is more realistic to briefly up-date short-, medium- and long-term plans annually.

The planning team will need to meet frequently enough to keep in line with whatever planning cycle is decided, although agreeing a workable planning cycle is always difficult as the academic year, the financial year and the annual central government spending round rarely coincide.

Phase Two: Auditing Progress

Step Five – Audit the present position

A number of whole-school approaches and techniques are available to the SPT to structure and support a progress audit. These include commercial packages like GRIDS (Guidelines for Review and Internal Development in Schools), but also much simpler techniques such as a strengths, weaknesses, opportunities and threats (SWOT) analysis. A SWOT can be conducted with the staff and governors wishing to identify whole-school quality issues. It can also be slightly rewritten and used for the review of academic departments or year-group teams in secondary schools, or by curriculum teams in primary schools. It should be remembered that this exercise will have more value if the participants have the opportunity to compare their perceptions with data gathered in advance by the planning team from other sources such as parents.

Another simple approach to audit is to evaluate progress using a pre-printed proforma containing structured questions. Typical questions ask:

- where are we now?
- where do we want to be?
- how are we going to get there? (what should happen?)
- what do we need/need to do to make it happen?
- how do we know when we have got there?

In reality, a full audit of a school based upon questions such as these would be too time-consuming, given the amount of change presently demanded of schools. For this reason, the Scottish Office Education Department (SOED) have suggested a basic framework for the audit which focuses on the **quality of key activities** in the school (see Figure 4.3). The framework is, in a sense, an outline 'job description' for a school and corresponds quite closely to the OFSTED inspection framework.

The school planning team would begin the audit process by evaluating the extent to which the school has achieved the goals identified in its current development plan. They would then conduct a limited number of specific quality audits of the school's work, guided by the audit framework outlined in Figure 4.3. The SMT might wish to nominate key areas of the framework for a

---

1. Quality of Pupils' Progress and Attainment;
2. Quality and Range of the Curriculum;
3. Quality of Teaching and Learning;
4. Quality of Financial and Resource Management;
5. Quality of Accommodation and Use of the Premises;
6. Quality of the School Community (Including Ethos, Support, Guidance, Community Links and Liaison With Other Schools);
7. Quality of Staff Management.

(after SOED, 1992, and OFSTED, 1992.)

Figure 4.3 A Quality Audit Framework for a School

more detailed audit if there were particular quality issues giving cause for concern—issues perhaps highlighted by market research conducted in the local community. The overall aim of using the quality audit framework is for the school to be able to produce a 'current position statement', which will determine the emphasis of future strategic and school development plans (see Chapter 6 for an example).

Although the modified SOED framework is used by preference in this book, schools may wish to use the 'Inspection Schedule' from the OFSTED *Handbook* as an alternative (see Figure 4.4). Again, the OFSTED approach provides not only a framework against which to audit progress in the school, but also convenient headings against which to identify specific future improvement and development goals in the strategic and school development plans. Unfortunately, the current OFSTED *Handbook* has a somewhat confusing sectional layout and is not as useful as a straightforward audit framework as it could be. The new OFSTED inspection framework applying from April 1996 should be less bureaucratic. With patience, the difficulties can be overcome and schools may find Chapter 7 useful in this respect.

Step Six – Identify medium-term programmes
The quality audit will produce a large quantity of data about the progress of the school. Before proceeding further with the analysis of the audit data, the SPT will also need to consider other factors which are likely to influence their proposals. These will arise from six main sources:

- the school's strategic plan;
- national policies, legislation and initiatives;
- the policies and initiatives of the LEA and the Funding Agency for Schools (FAS);
- factors emerging within the local community;
- existing school initiatives;
- the resources available for consolidation, improvement or development;
- the action points raised in an OFSTED inspection report.

This will provide the planning team with sufficient data to identify new programmes which more closely reflect **external demands** as well as **internal quality concerns**.

(Numbers refer to specific sections in the OFSTED inspection *Handbook.*)

(3)   STANDARDS AND QUALITY ACHIEVED
(3.1) Standards of Achievement
(3.2) Quality of Learning

(4)   EFFICIENCY OF THE SCHOOL

(5)   QUALITY OF THE SCHOOL AS A COMMUNITY
(5.1) Behaviour and Discipline
(5.2) Attendance
(5.3) Pupils' Spiritual and Moral Development
(5.4) Pupils' Social and Cultural Development

(6)   FACTORS CONTRIBUTING TO THESE FINDINGS
(6.1) Quality of Teaching
(6.2) Assessment, Recording and Reporting
(6.3) Quality and Range of the Curriculum
(i)   Content, Organisation and Planning
(ii)   Equality of Opportunity
(iii) Provision for Pupils with Special Educational Needs

(6.4) MANAGEMENT AND PLANNING

(6.5) ORGANISATION AND ADMINISTRATION

(6.6) RESOURCES AND THEIR MANAGEMENT
(i)   Teaching and Support Staff
(ii)   Resources for Learning
(iii) Accommodation

(6.7) PUPILS' SUPPORT AND GUIDANCE

(6.8) COMMUNITY LINKS AND LIAISON WITH
      OTHER SCHOOLS

Figure 4.4 Using Parts of the OFSTED Inspection Schedule as the
Basis of a Progress Audit

Step Seven – Evaluate alternative strategies for the use of resources

The planning team will then need to place their programme proposals before the full decision-making machinery of the school and co-ordinate a process which will:

- seek advice on strategies for implementing each proposal;
- systematically evaluate projects proposing alternative courses of action;
- obtain a preliminary costing of affordable alternatives as part of the budgetary process
- decide a programme of achievable priorities and their supporting projects.

Step Eight – Produce the draft school development plan

Once a list of priorities has been agreed in the school, the planning team will prepare a draft SDP using a structure similar to that suggested in Figure 4.5. The draft plan is very concerned with implementation and the approach suggested here is explained in more detail in Chapter 6.

To ensure that the draft SDP is focused on achievable programmes and projects, it is probably wise at this step to support

---

The school development plan should contain:
- Detailed programme goals in order of priority for the coming year and in outline for the next two or three years, which take into account LEA policies, central government reforms and the needs of the school and community, but extend beyond the curriculum.
- Programme and project action plans which include clear targets and standards; are fully costed; specify responsibilities for implementing, monitoring and evaluating progress and contain agreed, realistic task time lines.
- A clear indication of staff development and training needs which can be linked back to the appraisal process and the staff development policy of the school.

Figure 4.5 The Structure of a School Development Plan

the plan with **draft action plans**. This will further underline the principle that the development plan is intended as a working document for improving and developing the school, not as an ad hoc list of 'jobs to do'. The production of draft action plans also serves to identify more accurately the resources that are likely to be needed across the school and any problems of co-ordination that are likely to occur.

Step Nine – Consult before agreeing the final SDP

Once the draft SDP has been completed it is important that it is distributed as widely as possible. This will help to identify any potential difficulties and to gain final approval from the various stakeholders in the process.

Step Ten – Gain budgetary approval and allocate resources

Having consulted the various stakeholders, the SPT will present the draft SDP to the finance subcommittee of the governors and subsequently to the full governing body for final approval. The budgetary process is a crucial part of the decision-making process that underpins planning; it is the means of facilitating the choices made during the planning process and committing resources to the priorities recommended by the planning team (see Giles, 1995b). The budget links to the planning process through the following stages:

- budgetary review;
- budgetary forecast linked to a systematic whole-school audit;
- budgetary modelling informed by the draft SDP;
- budgetary approval of specific programmes of improvement and development that have the commitment of the staff and governing body;
- implementation of the agreed SDP programmes, facilitated by the budget and realised through a series of programme and project action plans;
- monitoring of the budget as progress is made towards implementation;
- adjusting priorities if the resources available in the budget fluctuate during the budgetary cycle;
- evaluating the success of the budget in achieving agreed targets.

It may be useful for the SMT to review the budgetary process at the beginning of the planning review to determine the extent to which it is integrated with the planning process of the school. Although the model is presented in a linear format, the various components are not isolated and may be taking place at different levels in the school at the same time.

Thus budgeting is a continuous cycle of activity which, if implemented without thought or care, can become simply a financial allocation process *masquerading as the planning process* in the school. Such a planning approach is flawed as it is resource-led rather than informed by educational aims and goals. Resources then are only seen in the limited sense of finance, rather than as the systematic allocation of time, people, equipment, consumables and use of the building. After all, many of the targets in the SDP do not require money, but do require the systematic allocation of other resources to the priorities in the SDP, for which there are always alternative uses!

One resource allocation technique worth considering briefly is the Programming, Planning, Budgeting System (PPBS) advocated by Caldwell and Spinks (1988). PPBS allocates resources against a series of detailed 'costings' of each planned programme of activity within the school. Programme and project priorities are determined by systematically costing alternatives, and then selecting those which achieve the goals of the SDP at least cost (ie effective and efficient). The previous spending pattern in the school is not taken as sacrosanct but resources are allocated to specific programmes and projects via earmarked budget heads within the budget and their use closely monitored and evaluated.

PPBS is certainly an interesting approach to resource management and is worth considering when attempting to move a school towards a more objective style of management which emphasises the link between planning and resources.

Once final budgetary approval has been received from the governors and the annual budget confirmed, the SDP can be issued so that action plans may be finalised and implementation proceed.

Phase Three: Ensuring Action

Step Eleven – *Implement programme and project action plans*

The final task facing the planning team is to advise on and support the effective implementation of action plans. This involves the use of the action planning technique discussed in some detail in Chapters 1 and 2. Action planning moves away from the informal ad hoc planning approaches so typical of schools in the past, by building into the planning process a means of controlling project implementation.

Action planning is in marked contrast to the kind of authoritative school planning in which staff are simply told what to do by a remote manager who imposes a plan without consulting, or inviting the active participation of, those who have to implement it. The essential principles of action planning are straightforward – objectives, targets and standards need to be discussed, negotiated and agreed if people are to be motivated to improve their own performance as well as that of the school. This is closely linked with the appraisal process presently being introduced into schools. Action plans also contain the means of their own implementation, in that they clearly specify who does what and when.

Action planning, then, leads to performance control *through* people, rather than *of* people. Consensus is achieved and sustained through a consultative/participatory style of management which aids communication and develops a sense of common purpose. However, management must be prepared to take remedial and, when necessary, firm action if policies are not implemented according to plan. It cannot be stressed enough that the ultimate test of an effective school planning process is the willingness and ability of management to take firm action when things are at a standstill or go wrong. Overcoming real or contrived barriers to implementation will be the focus of Chapter 5.

5
Managing Successful Implementation

SDPs are a rational approach to the management of change, but rational approaches are difficult to implement in people-driven and people-centred organisations like schools. Gaining commitment to produce a whole variety of plans in schools is not a major problem. Producing plans which become working documents that are actually *implemented* requires a level of awareness and degree of commitment from senior management and teachers which can be difficult to obtain in the present climate of change (see Chapter 1).

Senior managers will only persuade teachers to overcome their understandable reluctance to take on board whole-school planning if they can convince them that it offers recognisable and realisable benefits, preferably ones which reduce their onerous workload.

The purpose of this chapter is to explore some of the problems and difficulties encountered in the imaginary Northcote School where, as part of their pre-OFSTED review, the SMT decided that the school needed to introduce a more coherent approach to whole-school planning. The case study raises a number of management issues and includes some suggestions from recent research on managing change effectively in schools.

A FICTIONAL CASE STUDY – NORTHCOTE SCHOOL

Reaching a Decision
In July, the headteacher of Northcote attended a one-day conference on a whole-school approach to planning school

improvement. The examples of SDPs circulated for reference at the conference were of particular interest and very different from the LEA proforma that the school had hurriedly completed halfway through their 1990 academic year. In September, a management consultant provided some useful information during a school INSET day on OFSTED inspection, in which the importance of SDPs had also featured quite prominently. This was helpful to the pre-inspection review working party which had been established in the previous term. One of the SMT had also recently attended a short course on planning at the education management centre of the local university. The course had explored the role of the senior management team and suggested setting up a school planning team to manage a process of **strategic reviewing, auditing progress** and **ensuring action**. A summary of the key issues arising from the course had been circulated to senior staff. This included a stage-by-stage model for the successful action of a new SDP.

As a result of their discussions in a meeting that ran late into one October evening, the SMT decided to move ahead with a new SDP. They felt that the existing plan, which had not been revised since 1990, would certainly not withstand the OFSTED inspection due in twelve months' time and that it would also be very difficult for the school to produce *evidence* that a coherent planning process in the school was in place.

The deputy headteacher volunteered to recruit and lead a school planning team to produce the new SDP, and the senior management meeting moved on swiftly to the next item on the agenda without having considered the implication of their decision upon the *timing* of the existing planning cycle of the school.

RECRUITING THE PLANNING TEAM

In late October the deputy headteacher put a memo up on the crowded staffroom notice board asking for volunteers for the new school planning team (SPT). The team was scheduled to meet in two weeks' time in 'non-directed time'. In the week that followed, only three people signed the memo despite several reminders in morning breaks.

MANAGEMENT ISSUES 5.1 Make the Time
Insufficient time was earmarked by the SMT for a management review before starting to implement such an important whole-school initiative. From the outset, only superficial thought was given to **managing the implementation** of a new planning process and applying the principles of successful change management. Information about planning had been gathered incrementally; the school had been galvanised into action by the spectre of the impending OFSTED inspection and was *reacting* to an external need for accountability, rather than building upon existing good planning practice in the school. The governors had not been involved in reviewing the planning context with the SMT, neither had the staff been consulted or invited to participate in initial discussions before the new initiative was launched.

MANAGEMENT TIP 5.1 Demonstrate Commitment
Fullan (1991) stresses the importance of management commitment to any change—commitment *demonstrated* over a period of time, to give people the opportunity to adjust and reorient themselves to the new initiative. Schools in the Halton Board of Education, Ontario, Canada, involved in a school development planning initiative issued a *Managers' Letter* to all their staff, explaining the initiative and giving senior management's written, firm commitment to the change. A Managers' Letter for Northcote School is given on the next page, and is similar to the approach used in the **Investors in People** programme currently being promoted by local Training and Enterprise Centres (TECs).

THE FIRST MEETING

Although seven people eventually attended the first meeting, many key figures, including the headteacher and members of the governing body were missing. Those that did attend were not fully representative of the staff. The meeting lasted for two hours as no agenda or papers had been produced by the SMT in advance. As a result most of the meeting was spent reading through and

The Managers' Letter

Dear Colleagues,

The governors and SMT have recently conducted a **management review** of existing planning practice in the school in line with the OFSTED inspection framework. The review and accompanying staff surveys reveal a need for us to implement a more coherent approach to planning for change. This will help us to discharge more easily our statutory obligations, support existing good practice and deliver whole-school improvements and developments.

THE WAY AHEAD

Although we do not underestimate the importance of the forthcoming OFSTED inspection, we feel that to allow our pre-inspection review to influence our planning too much would be a retrograde step. We wish to continue to fulfil our vision for the future of the school and not be diverted from the policies identified in our strategic plan.

HOW YOU CAN HELP

Immediately after the half-term break in October we will be asking for a representative group of volunteers from the governors, staff, parents and students to join a small working party. In the first instance, the working party will be asked to make recommendations on how we should proceed with producing a new SDP. In the meantime, the governors and SMT will complete the review of our existing documents and planning process so that we can make an informed contribution to the working party.

OUR COMMITMENT

We see the planning review as a significant medium-term development project and are committed to:

- full **consultation** with all the various groups that have an interest in the success of our school;
- **representative participation** on all working parties in the decisions that will need to be made;
- creating opportunities for a free and frank **exchange of views** when difficulties arise in improving the quality of teaching and learning for our children, as well as the quality of services that we offer to our local community.

We hope that together you will be able to share *our firm commitment* to this new initiative over the next five years, as we gradually change the planning culture in the school.

Yours sincerely,

Headteacher   Chair of Governors

MANAGEMENT ISSUE 5.2 Getting the Right Team
Although well intended, the approach used for recruiting
the new school planning team was not very professional.
The SMT should have thought through, and carefully
planned in advance the launch of the new initiative, *before*
trying to recruit the new team. The SMT would then have
been able to communicate to the staff that this was a
major new development, with a long-term commitment
from the people at the top. Instead it seemed to be just
another school working party announced on the staffroom
notice board.

MANAGEMENT TIPS 5.2 Use Existing Strengths
The SMT should review the existing school planning team
before launching the new planning initiative. This allows the
SMT to build upon existing good practice in the school. The
SMT should also ask themselves a number of key questions
before the new planning team is recruited and meets for the
first time:

- Is the team to be a **representative group** and, if so,
  will it include governors, parents, pupils, and ancillary
  staff, as well as teachers?
- Is the team to be **selected** or **elected**?
- Will the team be an **advisory** group to the SMT, or
  will it have **executive** powers?
- What will be the '**job description**' of the planning
  team?
- What is a realistic **time line** for implementing the
  initiative?
- Who will be in charge of **co-ordinating** the work of the
  planning team and ensuring appropriate **liaison** with
  other groups in the school?
- How will the planning team fit in with the existing
  communication and **decision-making** process of the
  school? Does this need to be modified in any way?
- How is progress to be monitored and evaluated?

clarifying various points in documents given out by the deputy. No attempt was made to explain the brief of the new planning team or their role and powers in relation to the staff, senior management and governors. Even so, the meeting went well and there was some interest shown as the benefits of a more professional whole-school planning approach were explained and discussed. There was, however, general concern and much discussion about the implications of the forthcoming OFSTED inspection, with the spectre of accountability looming large. Minutes were kept by a volunteer from the group and a copy sent to the headteacher the following week.

AUDITING THE PRESENT POSITION OF THE SCHOOL

The school planning team decided to begin their task by setting up a small working party to carry out a school audit. The intention was to use the information from the audit to identify a number of improvement and development projects in a draft SDP.

The working party produced a simple **audit proforma** to be completed by all the curriculum areas in the school. Staff with particular areas of responsibility were asked to use the following headings to indicate:

- Where are you now?
- Where are you going?
- What resources do you need to complete the journey?
- How will you know when you have got there?

The proformas were to be returned within two weeks to any member of the working party.

Various obstacles to completing the audit proforma arose and members of the school planning team were approached individually for clarification and advice about the purpose and value of the exercise. Unfortunately, the proforma working party had not had an opportunity to explain the thinking behind the proforma to the whole school planning team. As a result, the advice given to the staff varied considerably.

It was now late November and in the run-up to Christmas, pressures of the season, tiredness and staff absence due to sickness were taking their toll. This was, of course, reflected in the quality of the proformas somewhat reluctantly completed by the staff.

The final proformas were eventually returned just before the last week of the Autumn Term. A school planning team meeting was called in the last week of term to collate the information received.

MANAGEMENT ISSUES 5.3 Create a Positive Climate

As the starting point for auditing progress in the school, the proforma triggered off a number of negative reactions in the staffroom concerning the timing, purpose and value of the exercise. Firstly, there had been no review of the planning cycle of the school. As a result the **timing** of the new initiative could have been much better. Secondly, there was little support for a new planning initiative because of the lack of **communication** from the governors and senior management. The proforma was the first real indication to many of the staff that a new planning initiative had been started in the school. Thirdly, there was a lack of **commitment** from the staff, partly due to poor communication, but mainly due to a failure to see the benefits of planning ahead when the educational scene seemed to be changing all the time. The staff felt that there had been enough change in the school and that right now their time would be better used preparing the documents soon to be required for the OFSTED inspection.

ANALYSING THE DATA

The planning team found that it was very difficult to analyse the data generated by the audit because the content and focus of the proformas differed so widely. Some were rather brief and pragmatic, dealing strictly with a list of jobs to do in a specific curriculum area. Others were somewhat philosophical and tried to take a broader view of curriculum development in the school as a whole. Some staff had returned incomplete proformas, whilst some had produced extensive documents based on the proforma headings, which were in a sense mini-development plans in their own right. With rare exceptions staff concentrated on resource issues relating to National Curriculum implementation. On the

---

MANAGEMENT TIPS 5.3 Do Your Groundwork

Use a preliminary questionnaire to assess the awareness and attitude of the staff towards development planning and to assess the extent to which the role of planning is understood by the governors and staff. This will give the SMT and school planning team a good idea of the barriers they will need to overcome before they begin the formal auditing process. An example of such a questionnaire is given in Chapter 7. The data from the questionnaire will allow the SMT to assess the **KNOWLEDGE, UNDERSTANDING, READINESS, WILLINGNESS** and **CAPABILITY** of the staff with regard to the new planning initiative. The SMT will then have a good idea how much they need to clarify for the staff:

- the **purpose** of whole-school planning;
- the **value of planning** even when the detail of government policy is changing;
- the **role of planning** in bringing about change which will make the school more effective;
- the possibilities for better **management of time** in the school as a whole if a coherent planning cycle is implemented.

---

whole, these were not prioritised or costed and where costings were given, they were of an administrative nature, mainly concerned with consumable stock, books and equipment. None of the proformas identified or costed staff development needs and linked them to curriculum development priorities.

The deputy head decided that the task of drawing together the main strands for improvement and development from the proformas was too difficult a task for a committee and offered to work on them over the Christmas break. A meeting for the full planning team was scheduled early in January to discuss the audit results.

MANAGEMENT ISSUE 5.4 **Determining Your Focus**
Because the planning team had not agreed amongst
themselves the purpose of the proforma and the precise
nature of the data that they were trying to collect, the audit
exercise was too open-ended. This meant that the team
collected information on a number of unrelated planning
issues, rather than data which could be aggregated and then
analysed to assess progress in the school. The planning
team was still not in a position to make objective proposals
for medium-term improvement and development
programmes in the school.

MANAGEMENT TIPS 5.4 **Clarify Intentions**
The staff should have been briefed that the audit was going
to collect systematic data for two purposes. Firstly, to assess
how well the school had been:

● implementing policies identified in its strategic plan and
● fulfilling statutory obligations such as the National
Curriculum;

Secondly, to identify a limited number of programmes in the
new SDP which would:

● maintain progress with existing initiatives;
● ensure continued implementation of national, LEA
and school policies;
● focus on specific 'in-house' improvements and
developments that are known to make schools more
effective (see Chapter 3).

IDENTIFYING MEDIUM-TERM GOALS

The school planning team meeting in January was more successful. The deputy head produced a document containing a summary

of the key issues for improvement and development identified by the staff. Although these were mainly related to the National Curriculum, a number of whole-school issues were also identified which related to:

- the availability of technical items such as computers, TVs and videos;
- the internal fabric of parts of the school building;
- a general lack of storage room;
- the allocation and use of teaching space.

The planning team felt that it was important to consult with the staff in the staff meeting scheduled for later that week. It was decided that the deputy should summarise the key issues identified by the audit and indicate the projects they intended to include in the draft SDP.

EVALUATING ALTERNATIVE STRATEGIES FOR THE USE OF RESOURCES

The consultative report from the SPT was duly presented to the staff meeting halfway through a crowded agenda. A few questions were asked by the staff, but no alternative proposals were made. On the whole the presentation was met with a stony silence, which was interpreted by the planning team as assent.

The following day, the headteacher spoke informally to the deputy about a telephone call from the chair of governors wanting to know why the school was planning things 'without having the common decency at least to mention it to the governors'. The head also reported that at lunchtime in the school playground, two experienced teachers with responsibility allowances had irately 'demanded' to know why their ideas for the SDP had been dropped. They had also questioned the 'decision' to include so many junior members of staff on the planning team and asked why the team was not more representative.

The deputy suggested that a representative from the governors and a couple of the more experienced staff should be included on the planning team. This was duly done, but morale was not helped when some of the younger staff were asked to step down so that the team did not become too large.

MANAGEMENT ISSUES 5.5 Think About Process

At this stage of the new planning initiative, the response of the staff and chair of governors was predictable. Poor communication, a lack of thought about the implementation process and lack of ownership by the staff were already slowing progress and introducing significant barriers to the future success of the initiative. The whole approach guaranteed that there would be no useful debate of the projects being proposed by the planning team.

MANAGEMENT TIP 5.5 Establish The 'Rules of the Game'

The SMT and SPT would have improved 'ownership' of the initiative by making a number of decisions clear to the staff from the outset:

- What was to be the **level and nature** of staff involvement in planning the future of the school?
- Which staff should be **members** of the new SPT and why?
- Was the role of the SPT to **advise** or **decide** on the medium-term programmes and projects to be included in the new development plan?
- Who should be **reporting** to the staff, the SMT or the planning team?
- Was the staff meeting part of a **consultation** process, or were the staff expected to **participate** in the planning process?
- Had the '**rules of the game**' been made clear to, and agreed by, all the players before the 'match' started?

PRODUCING A DRAFT SDP

Despite the changes to the membership brought about by the intervention of the headteacher, little in fact changed in the approach of the SPT. There was, however, a pressing need to get on with producing the draft plan as this was now expected for the next governors' meeting at the end of February. The planning team finally produced a draft SDP for consultation in late January.

MANAGEMENT ISSUES 5.6 The Tyranny of the Urgent
The planning team were trying to move too quickly into the stage of writing the plan (the tyranny of the urgent!). More time should have been spent seeking agreement on the programmes and supporting projects to be put before the formal decision-making body of the school. This would have allowed staff to have proposed a variety of projects for consideration and helped to ensure more long-term success in programme implementation.

MANAGEMENT TIP 5.6 Establish a Clear Process
The planning team should only produce a draft plan after they have:

- **sought advice** on the feasibility and desirability of the proposed programmes;
- **prioritised** supporting projects on educational grounds;
- **evaluated** alternative strategies for implementing programmes and supporting projects;
- **obtained preliminary costings** to assist in deciding affordable alternatives;
- placed provisional programme and project proposals before the finance subcommittee of the governors for discussion and **preliminary approval**.

CONSULTING THE STAKEHOLDERS

The draft plan was given to the governors, SMT and staff in early February with a request from the planning team for observations and written comments within two weeks. Ancillary staff, parents, pupils and the local community were not consulted. The memo accompanying the draft explained that any comments or representations would be taken into account before the draft went to the finance subcommittee of the governors at the end of the month.

Unfortunately, the proximity of the half-term holiday discouraged many responses from the staff, although the SMT did include an initiative on improving the marketing of the school. They were concerned about the falling birth rate in the local neighbourhood and the likely consequence of fewer children choosing to be educated at Northcote in future years.

THE FINANCE SUBCOMMITTEE

The finance subcommittee meeting at the end of February was able to consider the projected budget somewhat earlier than in previous years due to the government's unified budget statement now falling in November. With a 3 per cent shortfall forecast, budget projections were only satisfactory because fewer children were likely to join the school in September. It was not anticipated that there would be any need to increase class sizes, reduce staffing levels or adjust responsibility allowances to stay within budget. However, economies would have to be made elsewhere.

The subcommittee proceeded to approve the projected curriculum and staffing model. This had been modified in line with the staged implementation of the National Curriculum and the changes indicated in the Dearing Report (DFE, 1994). A modified staffing structure and distribution of responsibility allowances was also approved. The sum of money to be allocated for essential repairs to various areas of the school was reduced by 20 per cent, although the installation of anti-vandal lights at the rear of the building was allowed.

The draft SDP was then presented and considered. Expenditure items identified in the plan were approved, with the exception of a number of items of capital equipment which were considered to be somewhat extravagant in the present financial climate. Curriculum areas had their capitation cut by 15 per cent to help keep the school within budget. Unfortunately, the school planning team were not represented at the finance subcommittee meeting. As a result there was **no discussion of any of the educational issues** implicit in the items being discussed or the decisions being made.

MANAGEMENT ISSUES 5.7 Budget-led Planning
The budgetary process did not operate as a means of facilitating a coherent programme of planned improvement and development in the school. Items of expenditure were being considered by the finance subcommittee in isolation from educational issues identified in the strategic plan and SDP. The budget was not seen or used as an integral part of the planning process. The subcommittee was primarily concerned with financial, rather than resource management issues. As a result, major areas of resource management such as the allocation of staff and time in the school curriculum model, the rationale behind the distribution of responsibility allowances and the likely impact of 'across the board' cuts in capitation did not receive appropriate scrutiny.

MANAGEMENT TIPS 5.7 Match Plans to Budgets
The role of the finance subcommittee is to liaise with the school planning team to ensure **a match between the resources** available to the school **and the demands** made upon those resources from:

- the school's strategic plan;
- the statutory policies of the government and LEA;
- specific programmes for improvement and development identified in the SDP.

Caldwell and Spinks (1988) advocate the use of a planned programme budgeting system (PPBS) which is referred to in more detail in Chapter 4. PPBS **links** priorities identified in the audit process, **by means of the budget**, to specific programmes intended to maintain progress, or bring about specific improvements and developments in the school.

GAINING BUDGETARY APPROVAL AND ALLOCATING RESOURCES

The final version of the SDP was prepared by the school planning team and presented to the governors for approval in May. The budget was first on the agenda and the items approved in the subcommittee meeting at the end of February were discussed in some detail. However, one of the teacher-governors questioned the need for a 15 per cent cut in capitation and a 10 per cent reduction in the cost of the capital equipment purchases proposed in the budget. The subcommittee pointed out the need for a 3 per cent cut in the overall budget, and in general the governors were pleased at the way that the shortfall had been managed and congratulated the subcommittee.

The chair of the finance subcommittee then presented the draft development plan to the governing body and highlighted **expenditure items** contained in the document. The governors were assured that the intentions stated in the plan would keep the school within budget, and the plan was accepted. No discussion took place of the educational issues implicit in the plan nor the role of the governors in monitoring and evaluating progress towards its successful implementation.

The following morning, the teacher-governor reported back to the staff as usual on the previous evening's meeting. Although the need for a 3 per cent cut in the budget was already well known, the 15 per cent reduction in capitation and the removal of a number of items of capital equipment had only been a rumour. Morale was very dented by this announcement, coming as it did so late in the planning cycle. Staff, not knowing any of the details, were understandably concerned at how the cuts were going to affect their particular areas of responsibility in the weeks to come.

DISTRIBUTING THE FINAL PLAN

With the final plan approved, the document was desk-top published and issued by the SMT to the governors and staff in May. The final document included:

- the aims and goals of the school extracted from the school prospectus;

- a brief description of the history of the school; the number of pupils on roll and the number of teaching staff;
- a site plan;
- a copy of the school timetable and staff responsibilities;
- a subject-by-subject statement of the management issues to be faced in implementing the Key Stages of the National Curriculum and Dearing revisions;
- the development plan for dealing with whole-school issues identified in the audit, with development costs given in full;
- a copy of the existing budget, to be updated when final pupil numbers were known and agreed by the LEA;
- a proposed programme of staff development events for the forthcoming year.

MANAGEMENT ISSUE 5.8 Ensure Good Communication
The school planning team should be represented on the finance subcommittee by a member of the SMT to ensure that:

- the development plan is the focus of budget decisions in the school;
- educational aims and goals are properly considered in the budgetary process;
- decisions affecting the planning process are communicated to the staff and other members of the SMT so that priorities can be adjusted and confidence in the benefits of forward planning maintained.

MANAGEMENT TIP 5.8 Keep the Staff Informed
The planning team should have reported back to the staff with the outcome of the February finance subcommittee meeting. The draft SDP should have been constructed so that programmes and their supporting projects were in order of priority. These could then easily be adjusted during or after the budgetary process, without the need for 'across the board' cuts, which might even out the pain, but certainly maximise the damage!

Staff were asked by the SMT to start implementing the SDP from September. In order to do this effectively, the staff were asked to produce *detailed* action plans for their particular areas of responsibility, with help and advice provided by the school planning team. They were also told to go ahead with ordering approved capital items, books and consumable stock ready for September and that within the next 'couple of days' they would be notified of the precise amounts they could spend.

MANAGEMENT ISSUES 5.9 Will It Work?

As a working document the structure and content of the new SDP was inadequate. Although well intended, the plan:

- was largely descriptive, ie the site plan, school timetable and budget were presented without any apparent reason;
- copied the aims and goals of the school from the prospectus, without showing how these related to specific programmes included in the plan;
- listed curriculum and assessment issues as 'jobs to do' rather than agreed programmes for improvement and development;
- with the exception of internal decoration, did not cost the implementation of programmes and thus demonstrate how resources were being systematically used to make the school more effective;
- contained a copy of staff development events, rather than a fully costed staff development programme which would link appraisal targets with programmes identified in the plan;
- did not indicate *how* the plan was to be implemented, or give a time line with specific responsibilities for implementing specific action plans.

MANAGEMENT TIP 5.9 Evaluate Honestly
The final SDP produced at Northcote School certainly
looked good on paper, but the particular issues identified
above would make the plan very difficult to implement in
anything other than a very ad hoc way. (See Chapter 6
which provides an example of an SDP. It is also useful to
look at Chapter 7, which contains a section on evaluating
the SDP document, with tips gleaned from OFSTED
publications. This will help to avoid many of the usual
pitfalls which make actual implementation so difficult.)

IMPLEMENTING ACTION PLANS

The school planning team had a number of enquiries about the
precise nature of an action plan. At a team meeting in late May,
they decided that an input at the June INSET day would probably
be helpful to the staff and speed up the implementation of the
SDP. They prepared a number of documents for the INSET day
which explained:

- what an action plan consists of;
- the role of the action plan in implementing the priorities
  identified in the SDP;
- the importance of having targets and target time lines,
  checking progress and knowing when targets have been
  achieved; the value of the process in stimulating discussion
  and negotiating agreement on *how* particular targets were to
  be achieved.

Although the INSET day was a great improvement upon the
approach used to introduce the new whole-school planning initiative, the staff by now were distinctly unimpressed. To one of the
more vociferous groups in the staffroom, the need for staff to
discuss and negotiate with the SMT how targets were to be
achieved was starting to sound like a form of SMT control.

Another group of staff could not see the point of continuing
with the planning initiative. Their budgets had been cut to such
an extent that it was going to be difficult enough to implement
the National Curriculum, let alone the other priorities agreed in
the SDP.

MOVING FORWARD

The SMT recognised the danger signs and stressed that only a limited number of priorities would be implemented from the plan. They acknowledged that the new planning initiative had been a 'learning curve' for them all and opened up a frank discussion on where they should proceed from here. There was general agreement to the suggestion that the limited financial resources available to the school should be concentrated on the implementation of the National Curriculum in that planning year; that the SMT should work on a programme and supporting projects to improve the marketing of the school and that the staff should produce a programme and supporting projects to improve teaching and learning.

MANAGEMENT ISSUE 5.10 Focus on Success
The planning initiative was in danger of stalling as circumstances combined to defeat the well-meant efforts of the planning team. The staff needed reassurance that their work was still worthwhile and the SMT needed to provide a focus for *success* to maintain staff morale.

MANAGEMENT TIP 5.10 Limit Initial Demands
The SMT should go through the SDP and identify one or two whole-school improvements that would quickly gain the support of the staff and give them the success they needed to improve morale. The staff should be told:

● to focus their resources on the National Curriculum;
● that the budget and SDP would be linked in future years;
● that the SMT and staff should agree to produce one action plan for each whole-school development priority identified in the SDP.

CONCLUSION

Planning is not new in education. Development planning as a **holistic, consultative** and **participatory** process is, however, very new. Management will need to take time to understand and then manage the process of introducing an effective approach to development planning, rather than seeking simplistic solutions to complex problems.

Implementing a successful and on-going school development planning process is a great test of management skills. Managers will need to plan development in advance, create opportunities for discussion and genuine feedback, generate a feeling of ownership for the plan and negotiate mutually agreed performance targets with the individuals or teams that are going to carry out particular improvements or developments.

The move towards a culture where all staff have a voice and share in maintenance, improvement and development will take considerable time and patience. Management will also have to 'earn' the right to manage in such an interventionist way. Setting and agreeing a performance target is fine. Even regular monitoring of progress may not be too threatening. However, intervening and taking corrective action when agreed targets are not being achieved is something that teachers are more used to doing themselves than having done to them!

The willingness of managers to intervene and *manage* is the crux of successful whole-school planning. If plans are statements of what the school has agreed needs to be accomplished with the resources that have been allocated, then management have to take action when plans are not implemented. Unless this is a realistic option for an SMT, the planning approach recommended in Chapter 6 is unlikely to work effectively.

6
Examples of School Plans

School Development Plans do not exist in isolation; they are but one of several different types of plan which need to be closely *integrated* in a school if site-based planning is to be effective (see Chapter 2). For SDPs to be useful working documents they need to have emerged from a **strategic plan** which provides the long-term planning direction for the school. Strategic plans very much reflect the values, vision, mission, aims and policy goals of the school. The strategic plan is also evidence that the school is actively thinking about how best to use its resources to improve and develop the quality of its educational provision.

The school development plan, on the other hand, is the day-to-day **operational plan** of the school which, in addition to the **implementation of statutory obligations** such as the National Curriculum, prioritises a limited number of programmes and projects for improving and developing the school. Successful implementation of **programme and project plans** will involve the use of the action planning technique discussed in detail in Chapters 1 and 2.

The purpose of this chapter is to provide, in a case study school, examples of these three levels of planning and show how, in practice, they may be integrated by means of a 'School Planning Handbook'. As the content of real school plans will vary depending upon the particular circumstances of each individual school, the case study is presented mainly as a guideline for style and structure. Also, the contents of policy documents and plans included in the example of a 'School Planning Handbook' have not been completed in every detail, or made phase-specific.

As with other chapters in this book, management tips highlight potential problem areas in producing the actual documents, as well as providing a number of suggestions which will help make planning more systematic and workable. These tips have been kept to a minimum, to avoid repeating points made in other chapters, in particular Chapters 4 and 5. Reference in the case study to specific suggestions or to other key sections in this book are given in square brackets.

ANCASTER SCHOOL PLANNING HANDBOOK 1995–2000 – A CASE STUDY

The planning documents for Ancaster School are consolidated in the 'School Planning Handbook', which is openly available from the Headteacher, the Chair of Governors, the school office and the staffroom library. Reference is made throughout the Handbook to numbered sections in other relevant school documents which have supported our planning process.

The Handbook has emerged from a recent review of our planning process, which we initiated at the beginning of last academic year (1993). The review arose firstly because the senior staff and governors felt that we were well on the way to implementing the changes introduced by the 1988 Education Reform Act. The time was now right to identify improvements and developments which we *ought* to begin planning if, in the longer term, the school is to continue to serve our local community.

Secondly, a recent quality audit of our seven key areas of activity [see Chapter 4, Figure 4.3] brought to our attention a number of concerns which we *must* act upon. These concerns, and what we need to do to address them in the future, have been clearly identified in section B of the Handbook.

Thirdly, we commissioned some market research into our relationship with the local community. As part of our policy on staff development, data was obtained by two members of staff studying for additional qualifications at the local university. The data indicated that a considerable number of parents held negative opinions about a whole range of school issues. The results of the survey are summarised in Appendix A of the Handbook and particularly suggest that we need to improve communications with, and the perceptions of, our parents about the school.

Fourthly, the school will face its first full OFSTED inspection in 1996–7. An evaluation of our documentation by the SPT [see

Chapter 7] indicated that we need to thoroughly revise the nature and content of our existing planning documents.

Fifthly, the results of the school planning questionnaire recently completed by staff [Chapter 7, pages 103 to 107] suggest that we must review our planning process, in particular the approach presently used to identify improvements and developments that need to be made in the school. Staff clearly feel a lack of involvement in, or shared understanding of, what we are trying to achieve in our long- to medium-term planning.

MANAGEMENT TIP 6.1 Getting Started
Establish a '**School Planning Handbook**' to bring together
the various types of plan in the school. This reinforces the
point that all plans should be integrated so that the school
is 'marching to the tune of the same drummer'. The
planning handbook should be readily available and the
SMT should make frequent reference to it and visibly use it
themselves to remind people of the important decisions that
the school has agreed to implement in its plans.

For ease of use, the Handbook contains six sections:

- **Section A – The Ancaster Planning Process** – explains the planning process of the school; details the planning structure and decision-making machinery; briefly outlines the planning context at the time of writing; and highlights emerging trends and their influence upon present and future planning.
- **Section B – Current Position Statement of the School** – summarises the progress that we are making in our key areas of activity; discusses our successes and concerns; affirms our medium-term planning agenda; and suggests possible strategic directions to take with our planning in the future.
- **Section C – Strategic Plan** – contains a copy of the 1995– 2000 Strategic Plan, which was produced during the 1994–5 academic year.
- **Section D – School Development Plan** – contains a copy of the SDP for 1995–6, with details of our three improvement and development programmes and their supporting action plans. Planning priorities are also projected in outline for

1996–7 and 1997–8 to provide a rounded picture of what we have agreed to implement in phases over the next three years.

MANAGEMENT TIP 6.2 Small Steps Not Giant Leaps
Circumstances seem set for continuous change in education and, although policy has remained remarkably consistent in the past six years (see Chapter 1), there will be fluctuations in the resources available to schools for implementing their SDPs. It is advisable to complete the SDP document in detail for one year, but plan future priorities ahead of time so that these may be implemented or revised as circumstances alter.

- **Section E – Faculty/Departmental/Key Stage Development Plans** – contains the detailed development plans and action plans of individual faculties/departments. [In a primary school this section would contain the key stage development plans.]
- **Section F – Appendix** – contains data obtained from the audit process and market research, both of which have been useful in informing the school planning process.

MANAGEMENT TIP 6.3 Make Them Working Documents
So many school plans are too elaborate. They contain a wealth of information which should not strictly be in a plan at all. It is important to check that plans contain nothing which detracts from their key role as working documents. For example, it is not appropriate to include in the SDP a full budget statement for the school, nor to provide a detailed breakdown of the school refurbishment programme. Summaries *may* be needed to remind the reader of the context in which resources are being used systematically to improve and develop the school.

School Planning Handbook Section A – The Ancaster Planning Process

Responsibilities and Levels of Involvement
All governors and staff (including non-teaching staff) have planning responsibilities. Parents are also consulted and involved, directly through the Governing Body, and the Parents, Teachers and Friends Association (PTFA) and indirectly through market research carried out on behalf of the SPT. Pupils are consulted via the School Council which meets once a term and has a representative from each class.

The Role of The Governing Body
Governors normally meet once a term and are responsible for approving the policies of the school, as expressed in the Strategic Plan and progressively implemented through the SDP. They are also responsible for monitoring and evaluating the implementation of the SDP and for reporting the progress of the school to parents and the local community.

Governors are also involved in the committee structure of the school, where they have opportunity to make detailed contributions to the strategic planning process, as well as to the selection of development priorities to be implemented by the SDP.

The Role of The Senior Management Team
The SMT is responsible for advising the governors and the various committees concerned with the school planning process. In particular, the SMT is responsible for advising governors on the strategic direction of the school, suggesting appropriate long- to medium-term planning policies and confirming the viability of plans finally presented to governors for approval. The SMT also has overall responsibility for co-ordinating the school planning cycle, although detailed planning is conducted by the SPT which, at the present time, is an advisory group reporting directly to the SMT. The SMT also advises the governors on the statutory Annual Report to Parents and Annual Parents' Meeting, both of which will normally include reference to progress being made in implementing the latest SDP. When the inspection of this school

has been completed by OFSTED, the Report to Parents 'must include a statement of the progress made in implementing the latest action plan' (DFE Circular 7/93, p.9).

The Role of The School Planning Team

The SPT comprises the Deputy Headteacher (Chair); the Chair of the Finance Subcommittee of the Governors; elected representatives of the teaching and non-teaching staff; and a parent governor. [Secondary schools may wish to have their bursar present.]

The SPT meets once every half-term and all meetings have agendas and minutes, which are available for inspection in Planning File 2/95. Agendas appear in governors' papers and on staff notice boards one month before the next planning meeting. Minutes are circulated within two weeks of an SPT meeting taking place.

The SPT is responsible for collecting audit and market research data; preparing draft versions of the Strategic Plan and SDP; and passing them, with the assistance of the SMT, through the various school committees before final approval by the governors. The SPT is also responsible for managing the brief annual review of the SDP and the five-yearly update of the Strategic Plan.

The Role of The Teaching And Support Staff

The school is committed to a policy of full consultation with all staff as part of our planning process. There is participation by elected staff representatives in all planning committee decisions. In addition to the formal committee structure of the school, teaching and support staff may also participate in the planning process:

- through their individual contributions to the SPT;
- by means of agreeing to personal and professional planning targets during the appraisal process;
- in the production of action plans to implement the SDP when it has been agreed by the governors.

The Planning Context of The School

Ancaster School is a [age range, type of school and number on roll]. The school is located in the suburbs of a small city on the western edge of Shire County. The school mainly serves 'The Meadows', a large council estate built in three phases between 1955 and 1975. There are no major employers in the immediate area, although a small light-industrial estate provides mainly young female employment. Unemployment is 2 per cent above the national average and is significantly higher amongst single parent families and a growing ethnic population.

Other than a small local shopping precinct, there are few local services. There is a regular bus service to the city centre, although this is expensive to use on a regular basis. Unfortunately the out of town shopping centres and medical facilities, which are more convenient for local residents, are poorly served by public transport.

With the exception of the local schools, there are no public buildings large enough for the community to meet socially, and recent damage to the local scout hut and bowling pavilion has discouraged the local council from investing in much-needed community facilities.

Although housing is generally in good repair, the estate itself is not well looked after and suffers from considerable vandalism in the vicinity of the shopping precinct, in children's play areas and around the scattered blocks of garages located some way away from individual homes.

Car theft and burglary continue to dominate local crime statistics, but, although the 'soft' drug problem is growing, it has yet to be evident in school. Very recently there has been a marked increase in crimes against the person and teachers are starting to report more aggressive behaviour from parents, both at parents' evenings and when parents visit the school to see individual members of staff.

Teaching staff are also increasingly concerned at the extent to which problems in the external environment are manifesting themselves in the pupil's attitudes and behaviour. In particular, they comment upon the poor concentration of children in class, a lessening of respect for authority and a deterioration in basic skills such as reading, writing and the ability to express themselves orally. Lunchtime supervisors report an increase in violent or aggressive 'play' amongst the pupils.

> **MANAGEMENT TIP 6.4**
> Although not included here, it is important that the 'Planning Context' section of the Handbook also draws attention to **positive conditions** which exist in the local community. The school can then build upon these to achieve its mission. Likewise the 'Current Position Statement' section of the Handbook should briefly refer to and celebrate successes as the school proceeds with the implementation of the present SDP.

Section B – Current Position Statement of the School

Quality of Pupils' Progress and Attainment
An analysis of last year's SAT results indicates that the school is performing at slightly below the national average, but considerably below the average for the county as a whole. Some 10 per cent of our pupils are statemented, which is above both the national and county averages. Staff and parent volunteers point out that statementing is 'masking' full awareness of the fact that a further 10 per cent of our children are unable to read English fluently.

Quality and Range of The Curriculum
Although Ancaster provides a broad and balanced curriculum for our pupils, we have become more aware of the difficulties developing in our local community and the urgent need to review our curriculum. The time is now right to proceed with such a review, as the government have accepted the recommendations in the final Dearing Report (1994) which substantially slim down the National Curriculum. From August 1995 the National Curriculum can be taught to pupils aged 5 to 14 in 80 per cent of the time available and from August 1996 to those aged 14 to 16 in 60 per cent. The discretionary curriculum time thus created *could* allow us to provide a more relevant curriculum and also to enhance the opportunities of all our pupils.

Preliminary suggestions emerging from informal consultations between the SPT and the SMT, staff, governors and parents see an enhanced role for Personal and Social Education (PSE); the provision of more short-term individual support for particular pupils; and better use of new technology to create more interest amongst the children for mastering basic skills. However, the exact nature of our 'wish list' will also depend upon the overall curriculum policy of the LEA [or FAS] and the statutory orders and/or 'advice' that we receive from the DFEE.

Quality of Teaching and Learning

We have much to celebrate in the quality of teaching and learning that takes place at Ancaster, often in very trying circumstances. Yet discussions with pupils in the School Council and market research carried out with parents at last year's parents' evenings, underline a need for us to differentiate the learning experiences in our classrooms more effectively, so that we meet the needs of a widening range of abilities, without divorcing ourselves from the growing social problems to which our young people are exposed.

Although we are aware of the need for differentiation, a recent series of visits by the SMT to observe lessons revealed a lack of differentiation in a majority of the 40 lessons observed at the beginning of the last academic year.

Quality of Financial and Resource Management

Recruitment of pupils is stable, with 91 per cent of the parents of the new intake children having indicated to the LEA that Ancaster was their 'first preference school'. Although there is room in the school for numbers to increase by about 10 per cent, this figure is typical of other schools which serve the same housing estate. Numbers are unlikely to increase as collaboration, rather than competition, characterises relations between local schools.

There are currently [number of full-time and part-time teaching and support staff], a staffing level which still reflects the additional staffing support thought necessary by the LEA prior to the introduction of the LMS initiative. Salary costs reflect this historical position and, together with other fixed costs, accounted for 85 per cent of our delegated budget in 1994–5, which puts the school under considerable pressure to generate income from other sources (see 'Quality of Accommodation and Use of the Premises'). A full budget out-turn statement for 1994–5 and projected budget for 1995–6 will be found in Planning File 3/95.

With the advent last year of the new pay structure and different criteria for assessing teaching staff salaries, there was an opportunity for the governors to review the whole-school pay policy, staffing structure and weighting of responsibility allowances. The new policy, adopted for the first time this year, will increase the number of part-time positions and temporary responsibility allowances in the long term, as full-time staff leave or retire. This will reduce costs and increase flexibility as we endeavour to target curriculum support more closely to individual pupil needs.

Now that the final Dearing Report has been accepted by the government, as part of the 1995-6 curriculum review, we will be looking at how to use discretionary curriculum time effectively. It may be necessary to remodel our school day. This remodelling will be incorporated in the curriculum review and not shown as a separate programme in the SDP. The Curriculum Review Group have been asked to give this urgent attention as we have to give parents statutory notice of any change to the school day.

Quality of Accommodation and Use of the Premises
The school was newly opened in 1962 with flat roofs and, despite the addition of two classrooms in 1974, 15 per cent of our children are now taught in mobile classrooms, which are some way from the core of our facilities. We are fortunate in possessing a large school hall and excellent sports facilities; otherwise accommodation is far from ideal. Our recent rolling programme of refurbishment has been remarkably successful and over 60 per cent of our classrooms have been redecorated, carpeted and/or had curtains installed within the past five years. However, replacement of very dated classroom and dining furniture has been slower than anticipated, due to a costly increase in vandalism in the past two years. Anti-vandal measures paid for out of the 1994–5 budget have brought about a marked improvement this year and additional benefits are anticipated as the youth club, a partnership between the school and the LEA Youth and Community Service, begins to operate on the school premises at the beginning of the 1995-6 academic year.

Quality of The School Community (including Ethos, Support, Guidance, Community Links and Liaison with other Schools)
Ancaster is a thriving school and has been proud in the past of good relations with our local community. However, our self-image has been somewhat dented in the last two years as we have become something of a target for local vandals, many of whom must be former pupils of this school. We have to ask ourselves

why these events happened and question whether as a school we need to move beyond merely projecting a positive image to our local community and do more actively to establish more *tangible links*.

In addition to the medium-term community developments outlined under 'Quality of Financial and resource management', as a long- term goal the SMT and governors are keen to establish a 'parents' programme' and a trained 'Support Services Team' on the school premises as a *community* facility.

Quality of Staff Management
In addition to the comments under 'Quality of Financial and Resource Management', the governors and SMT are aware, from staff comments on their 'School Planning Questionnaires', that we have not integrated planning, staff appraisal and continuous professional development closely in the school. This year should see an improvement, with, for the first time, a fully costed SDP and the inclusion of a section on staff development and training. We have also incorporated as a long-term goal in our Strategic Plan, our intention to obtain accreditation as 'Investors in People'. The process of obtaining the IIP logo will address a number of the issues that have emerged from recent audits of progress in the school. These include integrating school and individual development needs with the planning process; the need to improve upon and integrate more closely our various levels of planning; and the need to review our approach to the planning process so that staff have a greater sense of ownership of the plans that they are expected to implement.

Section C – Ancaster School Strategic Plan 1995–2000

ANCASTER SCHOOL MISSION STATEMENT
'We seek to ensure that all children in our school develop their academic, social and personal potential to the full and grow into competent, tolerant adults who can work together co-operatively, manage their own lives and play their full part as responsible citizens and life-long learners.'

Ancaster School Aims
We aim as a school community to:

- generate a secure and caring school culture, where each individual is recognised as being of equal value.
- emphasise the social, moral and spiritual values and standards which make for good relationships in our personal and community life. These include self-reliance, responsibility, tolerance, honesty, self-respect, respect for others and their property and beliefs, courtesy, effort and self-discipline.
- develop a curriculum based upon the principles of breadth and balance, accessible at appropriate levels by all pupils through a variety of teaching methods and which caters for the needs and abilities of pupils and stimulates their learning.
- demand and celebrate the realisation of high standards of personal and academic achievement from all members of the school community.
- develop a distinctive local cultural identity by encouraging a concern for others and the environment through community involvement and close ties with local industry and commerce.

Ancaster School Planning Goals
In working towards achieving the aims of the school, our policy documents and long-term goals will focus upon the 12 characteristics of effective schools [see Chapter 3, page 28]. At Ancaster, we will strive within a collaborative culture to establish:

A COMMON MISSION
- shared values and beliefs;
- clear goals;
- curriculum leadership.

AN EMPHASIS ON LEARNING
- frequent monitoring of student behaviour;
- high expectations;
- teacher collegiality and development;
- an instructional and curriculum focus.

A CLIMATE CONDUCIVE TO LEARNING
- student involvement and responsibility;

- physical environment;
- recognition and incentives;
- parental and community involvement and support.

Ancaster Policy Documents
Reference may be made to Planning File 4/95, which contains the specific policy documents which have shaped the present goals of the school. Recent additions include:

- **Quality of Financial and Resource Management** – a revised whole-school pay policy, staffing structure and weighting of responsibility allowances;
- **Quality of Accommodation and Use of the Premises** – a new policy commitment to develop our spare capacity as a community facility;
- **Quality of the School Community** – a new policy on school-community partnership, working towards the introduction of on-site parent and community support services;
- **Quality of Staff Management** – a revised policy on staff development which emphasises accreditation.

A number of other policy documents are currently being revised or developed prior to approval by the governors:

- the school policy on sex education;
- the school policy on special education needs;
- the school policy on RE and collective worship;
- the school policy on equal opportunities;
- the school policy on exclusion and referral of pupils;
- the school policy for teaching and learning.

Progress in Policy Implementation
In the last Strategic Plan, our policy goals focused upon a number of initiatives, in particular establishing **a common mission**; beginning *to work together collaboratively* and the need to *improve the physical environment* of the school.

The 1995–2000 Strategic Plan has a sharper focus, with *an emphasis upon learning*. However, as outlined in the 'Current Position Statement of the School' ('School Planning Handbook', Section B), we need to place more emphasis in the longer term on developing *a climate conducive to learning*. This emphasis will

School Development Planning

need to be phased in towards the end of 1998 and will carry through to form the basis of the next planning cycle. Such a commitment to the future is subject, as always, to the outcomes of specific school quality audits and to any major changes of circumstance in our planning context.

Priority Goals 1995–2000 – an Emphasis On Learning

PRIORITY GOAL ONE – QUALITY OF PUPILS' PROGRESS AND ATTAINMENT

– to establish a school-wide programme for assessing, recording, monitoring and reporting pupil attainment and then act upon the results obtained from the programme to provide additional support, recognise achievement and establish incentives to improve performance.

MANAGEMENT TIP 6.5 Goal-Orientated Planning

The Strategic Plan provides the priority goals for the school and a few illustrative examples are provided here. Goals should reflect the aims and policies of the school; should be achievable and understandable and provide a clear basis for implementation in the SDP. Goals need to be specific enough to support action programmes, but not so general that the emphasis of the current Strategic Plan, in this case 'an emphasis on learning', is lost as the school development plan unfolds.

PRIORITY GOAL TWO – QUALITY AND RANGE OF THE CURRICULUM

– to revise the school curriculum model in the light of the 1994 Dearing Report and to use non-directed curriculum time as an effective vehicle for emphasising positive student behaviour and encouraging parent and community involvement and support.

PRIORITY GOAL THREE – QUALITY OF TEACHING AND LEARNING

– to evaluate the range of teaching and learning opportunities experienced by our children and to recognise and provide support for implementing 'best practice' in the school.

PRIORITY GOAL FOUR – QUALITY OF ACCOMMODATION AND USE OF PREMISES
– to continue our existing long-term strategic policy of developing a range of facilities and opportunities on the school premises in support of the local community. As a medium- term goal, we have included in the Strategic Plan our intention to use our spare capacity to establish nursery facilities in the school. This will help to enhance our role in the local community and raise additional revenue. Specific programmes will be initiated in the SDP within two years.

PRIORITY GOAL FIVE – QUALITY OF THE SCHOOL COMMUNITY (SUPPORT AND GUIDANCE)
– to review the pastoral support and guidance provided for pupils and parents, make more effective use of the resources of the school and external agencies and provide a level of service more appropriate to the changing needs of our local community. Specific programmes will be included in the SDP within two years.

PRIORITY GOAL SIX – QUALITY OF STAFF MANAGEMENT
– to obtain accreditation as an 'Investor in People' and in doing so to review the extent to which we integrate planning, staff appraisal and continuous professional development. Specific programmes leading to the award of the IIP logo will be included in the 1996–7 SDP.

Section D Ancaster School Development Plan 1995–8

Three programme priorities have been identified by the School Planning Team and approved by the staff and governors. The three programmes will form the basis for school improvement and development efforts over the next three years. The SDP for Year One (1995-6) is given in detail. Years Two and Three are also included in outline to ensure continuity between the Strategic Plan and operational planning in the school.

Detailed content of the year Two and year Three SDPs will be provided year on year, once our brief annual planning review in July confirms the feasibility of our existing commitments.

Ancaster School Development Plan, Year One 1995–6

PROGRAMME PRIORITY ONE – QUALITY OF PUPILS' PROGRESS AND ATTAINMENT

An analysis of the school's recent SAT results indicates that we are performing slightly below the national average, but considerably below the average for the county as a whole. Staff and parent volunteers have produced evidence that about 10 per cent of our children are unable to read English fluently. This has led us to question how effective we are in this aspect of our work.

We will develop a reading recovery programme as a model for assessing, recording, monitoring and reporting pupil progress. We will then be able to act upon the results obtained from the programme to provide additional support, recognise achievement and establish incentives to improve pupil performance.

MANAGEMENT TIP 6.6 Maintaining the Story Line

One of the problems with the 'School Planning Handbook' is repetition. At times whole sections, particularly in the SDP, are repeated as programmes are broken down into supporting projects and projects are broken down into **Targets** and **Task Time Lines** to ensure completion. An element of repetition is necessary to maintain the planning 'story line' and is one simple way of ensuring integration and continuity in the implementation process.

PROGRAMME PRIORITY ONE—ACTION PLAN

Programme Priority One will be supported by two specific projects:

- **Project One** will establish a reading recovery scheme in the school as a model for assessing, recording, monitoring and reporting pupil attainment and providing additional support. The programme will improve the reading age in the school from an average of [give existing figure] in 1994-5, to a reading age average of [give figure] within three years.
- **Project Two** will establish a whole-school approach for recognising pupil achievement and for establishing incentives to improve pupil performance.

PROJECT ONE TARGETS AND TASK TIME LINES
The project has been broken down into two **Targets** with supporting **Task Time Lines** to control implementation:

- Target One—recommend changes to school policy;
- Target Two—develop a reading recovery model.

TARGET ONE – Recommend changes to school policy
Task – to evaluate and recommend changes to school policy on assessing, recording, monitoring and reporting pupil attainment, with particular reference to reading.
Success Criteria – the final report to be completed and accepted by the governors in January 1996.
Resources – 6 x 1 hour meetings; 6 hours' writing time; 2 hours' training in project management and report writing by JTF.
Monitoring/Evaluation – JTF to monitor progress as indicated on the task time line for Target One. JTF to evaluate success in achieving the target and report to the SMT by 6 November 1995.

TARGET ONE—TASK TIME LINE	RESPONSIBILITIES
1 Establish a Project Management Team, first meeting 11 Sep 1995.	Team to consist of ARP, KAG and MJH.
2 Prepare and agree a draft policy report (maximum four sides of A4 paper) which makes clear, but brief, recommendations for the Programme Co-ordinator (JTF).	ARP to write. Team to present to JTF by 31 Oct 1995.
3 JTF to agree recommendations of the report with the SMT and modify as required after consulting with the Project Management Team.	JTF to meet SMT 6 Nov 1995. JTF to meet Project Team 10 Nov 1995.
4 SMT to present new policy to the governors for approval.	SMT present to governors in January.
5 Governors approve and Project Team to disband, with the exception of KAG who will liaise with other projects on the programme to ensure continuity.	

TARGET TWO – Develop a reading recovery model

Task – to implement the Reading Recovery Scheme as a model for the school in assessing, recording, monitoring and reporting pupil attainment.

Success Criteria – (1) achieve the deadline dates and activities specified in the Target Two time line; and (2) improve the reading age in the school from an average of [give existing figure] in 1994–5 to an average of [give figure] by the end of the 1997–8 academic year.

Resources – 6 x 1 hour planning meetings; 6 hours' report writing time; 40 hours' writing learning materials; 2 days' training for project team £100; supply teacher cover £300; reprographics £1000; one day's training for staff and volunteer parents £400 on the 19 Oct 1996 Professional Development Day.

Monitoring/Evaluation – KAG to monitor progress as indicated on the task time line for Target Two. JTF to evaluate success against the above criteria and report to SMT by 20 Apr 1996.

TARGET TWO—TASK TIME LINE	RESPONSIBILITIES
1 Establish a Project Management Team. Meet to determine the nature of reading recovery; establish training needs and information requirements in advance of Target One completion.	Team to consist of MRP, KAG and DSA. First meeting 12 Sep 1995.
2 Team to attend 2 x 1 day workshops on reading recovery at the Shire County Professional Development Centre. Complete 2 page summary report on training and circulate to staff, governors and parent helpers.	MRP to arrange training beginning 2 Oct 1995. DSA to write training report and circulate by 23 Oct 1995.
3 Meet to prepare an outline of resource implications of the project for Target One Project Team.	Team meeting 9 Oct 1995. KAG to prepare outline and liaise with Target One Team and Programme Manager (JTF) by 30 Oct 1995.

[SEE MANAGEMENT TIP 6.7]

MANAGEMENT TIP 6.7 Keeping Track
The Target Two task line above would continue in similar vein, including key dates to keep the project on track and ensure implementation. The SDP would then move on to the **Project Two Action Plan** and produce appropriate **Targets** and **Task Time Lines**.

RESPONSIBILITIES—Programme Priority One will be managed by JTF who, in addition to liaising with the SPT, will be responsible for:

- monitoring the programme and supporting projects *termly* and reporting progress in writing to the Headteacher;
- preparing a written programme evaluation for the July Governors' Report, based on the criteria agreed in advance and published in the SDP. In addition, the report will refer any emerging resource issues to the SMT and SPT in time for the brief SDP review in July.

MANAGEMENT TIP 6.8 Clarity of Layout
Space only permits a skeleton outline for the rest of the SDP and sections (E) and (F) of the 'School Planning Handbook' to be given here. As with the previous sections of this case study, the indicative headings and lead statements connect with the 'story line' running throughout and provide clear focus for action in the school.

PROJECT TWO ACHIEVEMENT AND INCENTIVES
The project has been broken down into [specify number] **Targets** with supporting **Task Time Lines** to control implementation:

- Target One—etc [see Management Tip 6.9]

MANAGEMENT TIP 6.9 Control Implementation

Use the following checklist to control implementation of the SDP and give programme and project plans reasonable targets and time lines for completion.

INFORMATION PROVIDED   **COMPLETION CHECK**

- Rationale

- Clear statement of what will happen

- Programme, projects, targets and tasks carefully integrated

- Timescale for implementation indicated

- Basis for allocating resources shown

- Performance targets agreed to enable programme monitoring and evaluation

- Responsibilities assigned

PROGRAMME PRIORITY TWO – QUALITY AND RANGE OF THE CURRICULUM

We will establish a Curriculum Review Group to produce the new curriculum model which we will need to incorporate in our SDP by the beginning of the 1996-7 academic year. Success of the programme will be determined by achieving SAT results for the school equal to the county average within three years.

PROGRAMME PRIORITY TWO—ACTION PLAN

The programme will be supported by two specific projects:

- **Project Three** will determine the nature of the new curriculum and devise a model for its implementation in the school;
- **Project Four** will determine the resource implications of the new curriculum model, including the staffing cost of phasing

in the new curriculum, modifications to accommodation and staff training.

PROGRAMME PRIORITY THREE – QUALITY OF TEACHING AND LEARNING
The programme will have an instructional focus and seek to enhance differentiation in our classrooms, with success measured in terms of a 5 per cent decrease in reported classroom behaviour problems and a 2 per cent increase in average attendance within two years of completing an in-house INSET course on differentiation.

PROGRAMME PRIORITY THREE – ACTION PLAN
The programme will be supported by two specific projects:

- **Project Five** – three professional development days will be set aside in 1995–6 to develop teaching and learning strategies which differentiate appropriately in our classrooms. Success will be measured in terms of a positive evaluation of the workshops, with training materials and booklet of teaching strategies to be incorporated into the staff handbook.
- **Project Six** – appropriate differentiation of teaching and learning will be incorporated into the classroom observation element of our two-yearly staff appraisal process in 1996-7 and 1997-8. Success will be determined by 95 per cent of lessons receiving a 'satisfactory' or above based upon the six-point lesson grade descriptions which are used during OFSTED inspections.

PROJECTED INPROVEMENTS AND DEVELOPMENTS
Outline of Proposed SDP, Year Two 1996–7
Subject to the outcome of the annual planning review, the school will continue to focus upon:
[details as appropriate for the school].

Outline of Proposed SDP, Year Three 1997–8
Subject to the outcome of the annual planning review the school will focus upon:
[details as appropriate for the school].

Section E – Faculty-Departmental/Key Stage Development Plans

MANAGEMENT TIP 6.10 Do not clutter with detail

Faculty/Departmental/Key Stage development plans should only be *summarised* briefly in the SDP so that the plan is not too unwieldy. However, their *detailed* plans should be reproduced here in section (E) of the 'School Planning Handbook'. These would be concerned primarily with the implementation of the National Curriculum and post-Dearing reforms, although there may be particular quality issues which have been highlighted in an OFSTED inspection, which require action plans which are additional to the whole-school development plan (see Chapter 1).

Section F – Appendix

This section of the Handbook contains data obtained from an internal audit of the school conducted on [give date]. There is also a section containing market research data obtained from a cross-section of parents by DJH and PAW on [give date]:

[details as appropriate for the school]

CONCLUSION

This case study brings together the ideas outlined earlier in the book and underlines the complexity of planning in schools. The approach used emphasises the need for the various plans of the school to be brought together in one Handbook. The Handbook aids integration and is a visual reminder that all plans in the school should link coherently, so that they may be implemented systematically within the constraints of the limited resources available. The actual plans should be straightforward and emphasise educational aims and policy goals, give a clear picture of what is happening in the school and community, and focus upon implementation.

7
Evaluating Your SDP and Planning Process

School development plans are a useful management tool for systematically improving and developing the school. Chapter 4 reminded us that at their best they provide:

- a vital link between the strategic thinking of the governors and SMT and the various action plans that are currently being implemented in the school;
- a clear indication that resources are being used *systematically* to improve and develop the school;
- a management framework for monitoring, controlling and evaluating successful implementation.

However, school development plans also require the support of a well-managed evaluation process to ensure that they continue to play a pivotal role in managing and sustaining change and improvement.

THE IMPACT OF OFSTED

Although Chapter 1 stressed the importance of planning for *improvement* and *development*, rather than preparing plans simply because of the need to be accountable to external agencies, OFSTED do require SDPs as part of their pre-inspection evidence. Not surprisingly, increased accountability has encouraged schools to review their SDPs and the way that they approach and manage their planning.

The purpose of this chapter is to provide an evaluative framework for such a review and suggest a *formative* approach to evaluation, which will help governors and senior staff to produce better plans and to work out the implementation and management of a more professional planning process.

Readers should note that, as a practical guide, this book is not concerned with the intricacies of evaluation. However, the formative approach suggested in this chapter helps to fulfil two out of the three purposes of evaluation. Firstly, there is evaluation *for* improvement, in which the existence and application of a systematic approach to evaluation leads to better practice. Secondly, evaluation *as* improvement, where the actual process of working through a formal evaluation process improves professional understanding. The third type of evaluation, is evaluation *of* improvement, which is not the focus of this chapter, but is referred to in the audit of progress discussed in Chapter 4.

Those readers who want a more detailed but 'user friendly' reference on evaluation, should consult the book in this series by Brian Hardie, *Evaluating the Primary School: A practical guide to the evaluation process* (1995). Secondary school colleagues may wish to consider the book by David Hopkins, *Evaluation for School Development* (1989).

HOW TO RECOGNISE AN INEFFECTIVE SDP

SDPs are not usually very difficult to evaluate. Even a very subjective approach can provide clear indicators of the quality of the planning process in a school. Problem plans that have not been supported by an adequate planning process are particularly easy to identify. They usually lack a number of the following characteristics:

- **COMMITMENT** – they have clearly been produced in a great hurry, perhaps due to lack of time, or an understandable lack of confidence in whole-school planning in a rapidly changing planning context;
- **UNDERSTANDING** – the construction, tone and content of the document suggest a poor grasp of the benefits of whole-school planning;
- **REALISM** – they are idealised and philosophical tracts, full of jargon and good intentions;
- **SPECIFICITY** – they are so vague that they could apply to any school and any set of circumstances;

- **SUBSTANCE** – they are largely descriptive statements of what is already happening, rather than what *will* be happening;
- **VISION** – they are pedestrian creations, more concerned with statutory obligations than whole-school improvement and development;
- **FOCUS** – they are aiming at too many audiences, including, amongst others, the LEA, governors, teaching staff, inspection teams and parents; accordingly they also lack
- **CREDIBILITY** – in that they attempt to do too much, and are not, therefore, achievable.

WHAT TO LOOK FOR IN AN EFFECTIVE SDP

On the other hand a plan emerging from an effective planning process is more likely to be:

- **INTELLIGIBLE** – the plan is an easily understood working document that staff will carry with them and use in their daily working lives;
- **PURPOSEFUL** – the plan contains clear priorities for improvement and development linked to specific goals;
- **REAL** – specific tasks for improvement and development are clearly identified and costed, rather than broadly generalised. Responsibility for carrying out specific projects is delegated to named individuals;
- **TIME CONSTRAINED** – target dates are specified and project achievement is capable of being monitored and evaluated;
- **INTEGRATED** – projects for improvement and development have emerged from a coherent planning process; there are clear links between the strategic plan, the school development plan and action plans;
- **ADAPTABLE** – the plan can be adapted and priorities altered to cope with unforeseen circumstances, such as time slippage or changes to the school budget.

Although general lists such as these are useful, they are somewhat subjective. There is a need to develop more systematic approaches if evaluation is to produce hard data which will help to improve the quality of planning in a school.

CAN OFSTED HELP?

Unfortunately, the OFSTED *Handbook for the Inspection of Schools* does not provide a coherent *framework* against which to evaluate an SDP or the planning process of a school. Items referring directly to SDPs and planning are inconveniently dispersed throughout the document. The more important references in *The Handbook* will be found in Parts 1, 4 and 5 concerned with:

- **'Efficiency of the School'**;
- **'Management and Administration'**, and
- **'Resources and their Management'**;

Readers should also refer to:
- Part 5 technical paper in section 6, p. 47 **'Financial Management of Schools'**;
- Part 9, **'Inspection Reports'**.

WHAT DOES OFSTED LOOK FOR?

Even a quick look at these five sections of *The Handbook* provides a useful insight into OFSTED expectations concerning SDPs and the role of planning in an 'efficient, effective and economical' school. Some of the key questions raised in the August 1993 update of *The Handbook* are included as examples in Table 7.1, but readers themselves should try to make sure they have the full picture, looking in particular at the revised OFSTED inspection framework in use from April 1996, and the three new OFSTED handbooks on the inspection of nursery, primary, and secondary schools.

OFSTED AND THE SDP

By bringing together the various references in the OFSTED *Handbook*, it is possible to adapt them as a *checklist* against which any SDP may be evaluated. Table 7.2 is an example of this approach, although it does *not* contain all the references to SDPs in *The Handbook*. However, the checklist is a useful starting point for a review and will enable the school to identify particular weaknesses. These can then be tackled by the governors, SMT and staff, using the approach suggested in Chapter 6 and perhaps they can even be included as priorities for improvement in the next school development plan!

---

1. Are the aims and goals of the school linked by the budgetary process to the priorities identified in the SDP, or are they separate documents/processes?
2. Does the school have a systematic process for matching resources to the priorities identified in the school development plan, or is resource allocation somewhat ad hoc and incremental?
3. Is the SDP a working document that reflects an active evaluation process, and is it linked to action planning?
4. Does practice follow policy, or are planning documents in the school full of laudable aims that are rarely implemented in practice?
5. Is it possible to trace a clear planning process through various planning documents, minutes of meetings and discussions with governors and staff?
6. Do the governors and SMT consult widely and facilitate participation in the planning process, or are plans the product of a limited constituency?
7. Have curriculum planning priorities been co-ordinated and brought together under the umbrella of the SDP?

Table 7.1 Some of the Key Planning Questions Raised by OFSTED *Handbook*

OFSTED AND THE PLANNING PROCESS

Evaluating the planning process is not as straightforward as conducting an SDP review. A similar checklist concerning the planning process can be adapted from the OFSTED *Handbook*, and Table 7.3 is included here for those who prefer this approach. Again, this is not a comprehensive list but, by concentrating on budgetary issues, it does illustrate the value of systematic evaluation.

There are, however, two problems with the checklist approach to evaluating process. Firstly, any assessor using the checklist will need to look at a considerable quantity of supporting documents

	Yes	No	Don't know
1 The school has an SDP.			
2 The SDP covers at least *three years* and contains an annual update.			
3 The SDP is based on a curriculum *audit* which analyses existing provision in relation to the aims and goals of the school and to local and national policies for education.			
4 The SDP indicates a sound evaluation of the school's existing provision and a clear view of what needs to be done in the future.			
5 The SDP sets down its main educational goals in order of priority.			
6 The SDP features the introduction and implementation of the National Curriculum together with arrangements for assessment, examination and accreditation.			
7 The SDP contains strategies for implementation which include: (a) staff responsibilities; (b) resource requirements; (c) time scale for completion; (d) clear goals and targets.			
8 Priorities in the SDP are broken down into specific costed programmes which also indicate the criteria for evaluating intended outcomes.			
9 The SDP clearly indicates staff development issues for the school and how these are to be resourced and implemented.			
10 The SDP indicates how implementation is to be monitored.			
11 The SDP indicates the arrangements for a periodic review and systematic evaluation of progress.			

Table 7.2 A Checklist for Evaluating an SDP

	Yes	No	Don't know
1 The governors fulfil their responsibilities for school development planning and management of resources.			
2 The planning process is allied to budget planning and closely reflects the aims and goals of the school.			
3 Planning (including development planning and budgetary planning) is carried out effectively so that appropriate priorities and targets are set.			
4 The planning process ensures that all available resources, including financial resources, are managed so as to implement the priorities identified in the SDP.			
5 Allocation of the budget reflects both the existing programme to which the school is committed and the priorities displayed in the SDP.			
6 The school works out the costs of its SDP and achieves a close link between policy, planning and the use of time, money and staff.			

Table 7.3 A Checklist for Evaluating Budgetary Aspects of the School Planning Process

which will assist in pulling together the threads of a school's planning process. These may not be readily available and are not always necessarily in compatible formats. Typical documents used by OFSTED for evaluating planning in a school are:

- the school prospectus;
- the school's aims, policies and goals;
- the school development plan;

- agendas and minutes of meetings, including governing body meetings;
- the latest budget out-turn statement and monthly profile, showing planned and actual spending against each budget head;
- staff job descriptions, roles and plans for professional development.

The second problem with a checklist approach to evaluating the planning process is the difficulty of writing statements which are objective enough to review evidence *consistently* and *systematically*. A more objective approach than a checklist is useful.

IMPROVING ON OFSTED

One objective approach which can be used to evaluate *both* SDPs and the planning process will be familiar to those schools involved in the Investors in People (IIP) initiative of the Department of Trade and Industry (DTI). This approach is quite capable of dealing consistently and systematically with a wide range of evidence and with large quantities of documentation. It focuses upon producing *objective* evaluative statements which are written in such a way that gaps may be identified during a 'desk-top review' of documentary evidence. This allows an assessor to identify a number of questions to follow up during a site visit and to check for conformance with agreed standards.

In the case of a pre-inspection review in a school, an internal assessor would use evaluative statements similar to those in Table 7.4 to check for conformance between the planning process and the production and implementation of the SDP. In this way a clear picture emerges of what *is* happening in the school, as against what *should be* happening. These discrepancies were at the heart of the problems in the Northcote School case study presented in Chapter 5.

In preparation for the introduction of an objective approach to evaluation, the school could ask itself:

- Are all appropriate supporting documents available?
- Do the documents meet with the expectations of the evaluation process?

1. There is public commitment from the governors and senior staff to the SDP.
2. Governors, staff, parents and pupils are aware of the mission and broad aims and policies of the school.
3. The purpose of the plan and their contribution to its implementation, have been communicated to all governors and staff.
4. The SDP is flexible, but sets out school goals and targets.
5. The plan clearly specifies how priorities are to be implemented.
6. The SDP identifies the resources that will be used to implement priorities identified in the plan.
7. Targets and success criteria are stated clearly in the plan.
8. Responsibility for implementing priorities are clearly identified in the plan.
9. Training and staff development needs are reviewed annually against the objectives of the school.
10. There is a process for evaluating the contribution of the SDP to the achievement of the school's aims and goals.

Table 7.4 Planning in Schools: Examples of Objective Evaluative Statements

- Do the documents provide evidence according to the criteria outlined in the evaluation statements?

As an example, a school, having given 'the implementation of the equal opportunities policy' as the first priority in their 1994-7 SDP, would need to check that:

- there was clear linkage between the SDP and documents containing the aims, goals and policies connected with equal opportunities;
- specific costed projects relating to the equal opportunities programme appeared in the SDP;
- the implementation of the programme and supporting

projects could be monitored and evaluated during a site visit by an assessor (conformance to plan).

EVALUATING THE EVIDENCE

To make the task of evaluation more manageable, the assessor could use a simple gap analysis proforma which is adapted from the IIP *Assessor's Workbook* (see Table 7.5). The assessor would then use criteria similar to those given in Table 7.4 to evaluate the documentary evidence presented by the school to record:

- the actual evidence considered;
- any gaps identified;
- the questions/issues to probe in the school;
- the person to whom questions should be addressed;
- the subsequent results of any enquiries.

FOLLOWING THROUGH

If we take the example of the planning process used to produce the SDP at Northcote School (see Chapter 5), the assessor would have identified a number of gaps during the desk-top review of documentary evidence. Some of these gaps are used as illustrations in Table 7.5.

Having identified the gaps in the documentary evidence, the assessor would need to establish whether these were omissions in the *documents*, or actually omissions in *practice*. This is achieved by tracking particular issues, identified by the assessor, through the planning process of the school. A report is then produced of particular action points that require management attention.

THE ASSESSOR'S REPORT

The assessor's report should be brief and based on the evidence obtained from the desk-top review and tracking exercise. In the case of the Northcote School, any report obtained using the approaches suggested in this chapter would be far more comprehensive than the somewhat brief paragraphs characteristic of the new OFSTED inspection report. Certainly Northcote School would need to establish:

EVIDENCE CONSULTED
Document 1—school prospectus
Document 2—the school mission statement
Document 3—the aims and goals of the school
Document 4—the SDP
Document 5—minutes of the governing body; finance sub-committee and school planning team
Document 6—summary of the school budget

PAGE	GAPS	ISSUES TO PROBE	WHO TO ASK	ANSWERS
SDP, page 1	School aims and goals do not match SDP priorities.	When were the aims and goals of the school last updated?	Head & Chair of Governors	1986
SDP, page 3	No connection is indicated between the strategic thinking of the governors and SMT and the pupil numbers and staffing figures in the plan.	What are pupil projections for the future? How do these affect future staffing levels?	Head Deputy Head	No data
SDP	No description of the planning process in the school included in the SDP.	Who was involved in producing the SDP? Was there consultation/ participation?	Cross-section of staff, parents and governors	Process not clear to staff and governors
SDP	The staff development programme does not relate to the priorities indicated in the SDP.	Check staff development records. Is there an appraisal process functioning?	Deputy Head Deputy Head	No records Well-managed process but not linked to SDP.

Table 7.5 The Planning Process – Gap Analysis Proforma

- clear, up-to-date aims and goals which reflect the strategic plan for the future of the school;
- a clear link between the aims and goals of the school and the SDP;
- a planning process which has been shared with and understood by everyone in the school community;
- clear planning systems and structures to support the planning process;
- an explicit cycle of planning and budgetary activity, where the budget is seen as a means of implementing the priorities identified in the SDP;
- clear costed priorities;
- a link between the staff appraisal process and the school development plan so that staff development and organisational development are explicitly linked;
- action plans with targets, timescales and named people with the responsibility and *power* to act;
- real knowledge of the existing situation based on targeted audits which consider a range of issues regarding **quality** in addition to the curriculum;
- a clear perception of the desired outcomes.

AN ALTERNATIVE APPROACH

Those who do not like using assessors and evaluative statements in an approach which evaluates *for* improvement, can use a *structured questionnaire* instead (see Table 7.6). This approach to evaluation is an example of evaluation *as* improvement, where the process of working through the questionnaire, gathering the data and analysing the results helps to inform, educate and improve professional practice.

The questionnaire is very user-friendly and should take about five minutes to complete. It is self-explanatory, yet pertinent, as the questions have been drawn up using both the OFSTED *Handbook* and a wide range of development planning literature. It is also easy to modify and include in any existing approach to evaluation that a school may already have in place. The questionnaire is only effective if completed *without reference to the actual planning documents of the school.*

TABLE 7.6 School Planning Questionnaire

1. Does your school have a strategic plan?

(a) YES	(b) NO	(c) DON'T KNOW

2. Does your school have a school development plan?

(a) YES	(b) NO	(c) DON'T KNOW

3. Does the planning process in your school make clear the difference between strategic planning and development planning?

(a) YES	(b) NO	(c) DON'T KNOW

4. In which one of the following academic years was your school development plan last formally updated:

(a) 1991-2	(d) 1994–5	(g) DON'T KNOW
(b) 1992-3	(e) 1995–6	(h) BEFORE MY TIME
(c) 1993-4	(f) 1996–7	(i) ANNUAL UPDATE

5. Who was involved in producing the development plan in your school? Please tick one or more from:

(a) LEA Adviser	(e)Head	(i) Deputy Head
(b) Governors	(f) Allowance holders	(j) Don't know
(c) Teachers	(g) Parents	(k) Before my time
(d) Pupils	(h) Ancillary staff	

6. Were you involved in producing the school development plan?

(a) YES	(b) NO

7. Do you have a copy of your latest school development plan?

(a) YES	(b) NO

8. What are the whole-school improvement and development programmes agreed in this year's school development plan?

(a)

_____

_____

_____

or (b) don't know _____ ☐

9. Does your school development plan:
(i) contain a summary of the *recent* aims and goals of the school?

(a) YES	(b) NO	(c) DON'T KNOW

(ii) contain clear costed priorities for development?

(a) YES	(b) NO	(c) DON'T KNOW

(iii) link staff development priorities identified during the appraisal process to the programme priorities in the school development plan?

(a) YES	(b) NO	(c) DON'T KNOW

(iv) contain an indication of how staff development priorities are to be met?

(a) YES	(b) NO	(c) DON'T KNOW

10. Does your school have action plans which demonstrate that national, local and school priorities are being systematically resourced and implemented?

(a) YES	(b) NO	(c) DON'T KNOW

If your answer to 10 is YES proceed with question 11.
If your answer is NO or DON'T KNOW please move on to question 18.

11. Do your action plans link to specific programmes prioritised in the school development plan?

(a) YES	(b) NO	(c) DON'T KNOW

12. Do your action plans contain clear success criteria?

(a) YES	(b) NO	(c) DON'T KNOW

13. Do your action plans indicate a timescale for implementation?

(a) YES	(b) NO	(c) DON'T KNOW

14. Do your action plans allocate responsibility to named staff for completion?

(a) YES	(b) NO	(c) DON'T KNOW

15. Do your action plans focus solely on curriculum issues?

(a) YES	(b) NO	(c) DON'T KNOW

16. Do your action plans indicate who will monitor/evaluate progress?

(a) YES	(b) NO	(c) DON'T KNOW

17. Do your action plans indicate when monitoring/evaluation is to occur?

(a) YES	(b) NO	(c) DON'T KNOW

18. Do you have a job description? **If NO or DON'T KNOW go to question 20.**

(a) YES	(b) NO	(c) DON'T KNOW

19. Does your job description specifically state your responsibilities for any aspect of planning in the school?

(a) YES	(b) NO

20. From each pair of statements tick one that most closely describes the management of planning in your school.

(a) Plans are produced by a formal planning process.
(b) Plans are produced by an ad hoc process.

(c) Plans are closely linked and integrated with each other in the school.
(d) Plans exist throughout the school, but are not closely linked and integrated with each other.

(e) There is an obvious planning cycle in the school.
(f) There is no obvious planning cycle in the school.

(g) The planning process in the school is systematically linked to the annual budgeting process.
(h) The planning process in the school is not systematically linked to the annual budgeting process.

(i) There is systematic evaluation of progress in achieving whole-school targets.
(j) There is no systematic evaluation of progress in achieving whole-school targets.

(k) The programmes for improvement and development in our school development plan are concerned with more than implementing the National Curriculum.

(l) The programmes for improvement and development in our school development plan are only concerned with implementing the National Curriculum.

INTERPRETING THE RESULTS OF THE QUESTIONNAIRE

It should be remembered that the results obtained by questionnaires are the *perceptions* of governors and teachers. If a pattern of answers is repeated by a number of respondents, then aspects of the planning process in the school clearly need to be reconsidered. Even if the respondents are mistaken, it probably indicates, as in the Northcote case study, that communication is not as good as the SMT thought it to be.

QUESTIONNAIRE RESULTS

Rather than invent results for the fictitious Northcote School, a sample of the actual results recently obtained from a convenience survey of teaching staff in 106 primary and secondary schools are summarised in Table 7.7. Although not generalisable to all schools, the sample of results clearly indicates the potential of questionnaires as a means of evaluating planning in a school.

The results in Table 7.7 indicate considerable gaps in current practice. Although further research is required, in too many of the cases surveyed:

- planning is ad hoc and incremental, with little whole-school planning taking place;
- schools are reacting to change rather than taking strategic responsibility for future improvements and developments;
- there is little *conscious* link between the aims and policies in the strategic plan, and the priority goals identified in the SDP;
- the SDP is still in effect a list of 'jobs to do', rather than a list of agreed priorities which are being systematically resourced and implemented to improve and develop the school;
- there does not seem to be any systematic evaluation of the progress towards policy implementation, or gathering of hard data on which to base future planning decisions.

These are serious issues, but are unlikely to be addressed professionally in the current climate if schools allow their planning to be dominated by the spectre of OFSTED, or driven *in the first instance* by their budget.

	Abbreviated Questions and statements	Positive Results as a percentage
1.	Does your school have a strategic plan?	45
2.	Does your school have an SDP?	88
3.	The planning process makes the difference between strategic and development planning clear.	21
4.	Were governors involved in producing your SDP?	31
5.	Were parents involved in producing your SDP?	5
6.	Do you have a copy of your latest SDP?	69
7.	Staff who knew their SDP priorities for 1993-4.	59
8.	The SDP contains clear costed priorities for development.	31
9.	Does your school have action plans?	58
10.	Plans are produced by a formal planning process.	59
11.	Plans are produced by an ad hoc process.	41
12.	Plans are closely linked and integrated in the school.	44
13.	Plans exist in the school, but are not closely linked.	55
14.	There is an obvious planning cycle in the school.	45
15.	There is no obvious planning cycle in the school.	55
16.	Planning is closely linked to the annual budgeting process.	56
17.	Planning is not closely linked to the annual budgeting process.	44
18.	Progress in achieving whole-school targets is systematically evaluated.	30
19.	Progress in achieving whole-school targets is not systematically evaluated.	70

(Giles, 1995a).

Table 7.7 School Planning Questionnaire Sample Results

CONCLUSION

OFSTED is already having a considerable impact upon shaping the planning process and SDP in some schools. Not only are schools required to produce specific documents relating to planning, but they must also be able to produce them in a form that provides *evidence* that the documents have emerged from a coherently managed planning process.

As yet the OFSTED process, the guidance documents and the support available to schools are less than perfect. However, the OFSTED working slogan of 'inspection *for* improvement' underlines their desire for quality assurance rather than quality control. Schools that prepare in advance for inspection, evaluate as a routine part of the life of the school and sensibly use the clues in OFSTED publications will be taking part in a process of *quality assurance.* Schools that over-react to inspection by disrupting their day-to-day work, thus creating an artificial response to what they perceive as an external threat, are subjecting themselves to a four-year cycle of *quality control.*

The intention of the formative approach to evaluation proposed in this chapter has been to use the clues from OFSTED, the work of IIP and information from research to help schools establish a quality assurance approach to improving existing practice. This will enable schools more easily to assume the responsibility for strategic planning emphasised in recent legislation and to take OFSTED inspections in their stride.

Using the OFSTED experience as an opportunity radically to rethink and professionalise planning will be more important in the long-term for ensuring the strategic future of a school.

8
Planning and the Future

The purpose of this book is to provide a practical management guide for schools wishing to review their plans and planning process. The book is based on the principle that whole-school development planning is concerned with co-ordinating and sustaining change in order to improve the quality of individual schools. Good planning:

- provides a school's vision and mission;
- clarifies the aims, policies and goals of the school;
- brings together the short-, medium- and long-term development priorities;
- provides a process for the management of change that facilitates planning and decision-making, provides a means of monitoring and evaluation progress and, lastly,
- acts as a basis for external inspection.

In practical terms, 'good' planning must also provide an approach for co-ordinating the changes necessary to implement government policy. This is not easy, owing to the task-orientated nature of much of the work of school management and perhaps an understandable tendency to 'wait and see' what the government will legislate next!

RECOGNISING POLICY TRENDS

The real danger in schools' adopting the 'wait and see' approach to planning is that teachers are not clear *what* they have to do, *why* they have to do it, or *when* it has to be done. Planning in such circumstances tends to be a form of 'incremental *adhocracy*'. The following passage underlines the importance of the strategic

110

management of the future as schools face the second wave of educational reform introduced in recent legislation:

> 'There were four people named Everybody, Somebody, Anybody and Nobody. There was an important job to be done and Everybody was asked to do it. Everybody was sure that Somebody would do it. Anybody could have done it, but Nobody did it. Somebody got angry about that, because it was Everybody's job. Everybody thought Anybody could do it but Nobody realised that Everybody wouldn't do it. It ended up that Everybody blamed Somebody when Nobody did what Anybody could have done'
>
> (Everard, 1986).

However, developing a strategic view of (the remarkably consistent) educational *policy* in recent years does provide a useful basis for anticipating the likely planning demands to be made on schools in the future. The alternative is not to treat planning seriously and to be for ever *reacting* to change, which is stressful to all concerned, as well as wasteful of time and other resources.

PLANNING AND THE FUTURE

Reference has been made throughout this book to the fact that OFSTED is not always happy with the current planning situation in schools. As further legislation in the UK enhances independence, choice, competition and accountability in a market-driven educational system, evidence of the lack of a coherent planning process in schools casts doubt on their ability to operate successfully in a decentralised environment.

It is hardly surprising, therefore, that there have been indications that planning in schools could become more prescribed and necessarily take on a more significant role in the near future. Three examples will serve to illustrate this trend.

THE EXAMPLE OF FURTHER EDUCATION

With the changes to further education introduced by the 1992 Education Act, FE became independent from LEA control in April 1993. Funding arrangements for the FE sector are now managed by the Further Education Funding Council (FEFC) which has made proposals for a two-stage approach to strategic planning (*Times Higher Education Supplement*, 14 August 1992). The initial planning phase is:

'. . . aimed at assisting college management as well as forming the basis for the Further Education Council's bids for public money, for accountability of funds and for securing adequate provision. The council might also use the plans to gather overall information on the new sector and to monitor trends.'

The focus of the first stage will require colleges to provide limited information about themselves, decide their mission and begin to look at their longer-term development. Stage two will be far more comprehensive:

'It will probably incorporate an in-depth analysis of objectives and their delivery over a period of three to five years, a detailed examination of college intentions, accommodation plans and an analysis of a wide range of activities. There will also be analysis of human resource needs and their ability to match academic developments and plans to assure and assess quality.'

The FEFC will also be responsible for managing Grants for Educational Support and Training (GEST) for the sector, previously one of the major residual activities of LEAs.

THE EXAMPLE OF THE FUNDING AGENCY

A parallel can be construed between the impact of the 1992 Act on FE and the likely impact of the 1993 Education Act which established the Funding Agency for Schools (FAS). The FAS is intended as a means of providing a coherent funding regime for schools that have opted out of LEA control. As more schools opt out of local authority control, the demise of LEAs will accelerate to the point where there will no longer be any need for an Education Committee. Schools will be funded largely on a national LMS funding formula administered by a local FAS to the level of the Standard Spending Assessment (SSA).

It is likely that similar arrangements to those of the FEFC will apply, in that the FAS will administer GEST funding as well as seed corn funding for specific projects that central government wishes to see introduced quickly in the school sector. It would also be possible for the FAS to administer supplementary 'quality payments' to schools on achieving 'outcome-based' performance targets determined by the FAS, with perhaps an additional bonus linked to a successful OFSTED inspection.

In the case of schools, development plans will increasingly become a focus as this model of resourcing schools develops. Funding at the moment rewards successful schools somewhat crudely, in that resources follow pupil numbers. Resources are in no way tied to quality of teaching and learning, cost effectiveness, or, as in TECs, the success rate of students obtaining vocational qualifications.

The FAS will present an opportunity to establish additional funding criteria for schools to drive and implement government policy through means other than the weighted pupil number driven LMS formula. Quite clearly there is an inevitable move towards a funding regime where at least an element of **school funding will follow the SDP and its successful implementation**, success being monitored and evaluated by OFSTED inspection teams.

THE EXAMPLE OF CHOICE AND DIVERSITY

The recent thinking of the UK government, outlined in the White Paper *Choice and Diversity* (HMSO, 1992) and legislated in the 1993 Education Act, has already been referred to in Chapter 1. It is worth repeating by way of a conclusion, particularly in relation to the concept of 'funding following plan'.

This Act has considerably enhanced the autonomy of schools by allowing them to apply to:

- change their character;
- specialise in terms of curriculum;
- select pupils by ability.

In addition, schools will need to assess other strategic implications of the Act, including the gradual demise of LEAs and their likely replacement from April 1994 by the FAS. There are also open discussions in the media over the introduction of voucher schemes and renewed pressures from central government for schools to opt out of LEA control and elect for centrally funded grant maintained status.

Within these very clear centrally determined policy parameters, schools will have to decide *individually* the type of school that they intend to become and plan the range of services that they intend to provide for their various client groups.

If schools are to grasp the strategic initiative offered by further decentralisation, they will need to avoid resisting change and think beyond OFSTED towards determining their own strategic future in the increasingly competitive educational marketplace (see Giles 1995c).

CONCLUSION

If whole-school planning is to overcome resistance to change and be accepted as a successful antidote to existing practice, it is important for senior managers in schools to focus their planning efforts upon universal truths which are important to teachers. There is little point in adopting poorly grasped planning concepts if whole-school planning is to continue to gain credibility as a sustainable approach for managing improvement and development. This is most easily accomplished through a planning process which delivers improved educational opportunity for children and commands the understanding, commitment and support of the teaching profession.

Glossary of Acronyms

DES Department of Education and Science.

DFE Department for Education.

DFEE Department for Education and Employment.

DTI Department of Trade and Industry.

FAS Funding Agency for Schools.

FEFC Further Education Funding Council, the government appointed body responsible for allocating resources and monitoring resource planning and utilisation in the FE sector.

GEST Grants for Educational Support and Training, funding from central government to LEAs for specific areas of INSET (eg records of achievement) and for books, equipment and ancillary staff in support of specific developments.

GMS Grant Maintained School, a self-governing school which has opted out of local authority control and is directly funded by the DFE.

HMI Her Majesty's Inspectors (of schools).

IIP Investors in People, a DTI sponsored quality assurance approach which links the development needs of individuals and the organisation through a systematic approach to planning and staff development. Organisations producing evidence of a coherent IIP approach are awarded the IIP laurel wreath logo.

INSET In-Service Education for Teachers.

LEA Local Education Authority.

LMS Local Management of Schools, the arrangements by which LEAs delegate to individual schools responsibility for financial and other aspects of management.

OFSTED Office for Standards in Education, the independent arm of government responsible for inspecting schools under the terms of the 1992 Education Act.

PPBS Programming, Planning, Budgeting System, a means of deciding programme priorities in the school and allocating sufficient resources.

PTFA Parents, Teachers and Friends Association, voluntary grouping of parents, teachers and friends who support the school in a variety of ways.

SAT Standard Assessment Tests, external National Curriculum assessments which incorporate a variety of assessment methods depending on the subject and Key Stage.

SDP School Development Plan.

SMT Senior Management Team, usually the senior staff of the school working together collaboratively.

SOED Scottish Office Education Department.

SPT School Planning Team.

SSA Standard Spending Assessment, the government's assumed (as against actual) level of spending required by a local authority to maintain services, including education.

SWOT Strengths, Weaknesses, Opportunities and Threats, a simple technique for beginning an internal quality audit in a school.

TEC Training and Enterprise Council, local training organisations sponsored by the DTI.

Further Reading

Beare, H., Caldwell, B. J. and Millikan, R.H. (1989) *Creating an Excellent School: Some New Management Techniques.* London: Routledge.

Caldwell, B. J. and Spinks, J. M. (1988) *The Self-Managing School.* London: Falmer Press.

DEPARTMENT OF EDUCATION AND SCIENCE (1988) *Local Management of Schools*, Circular 7/88. London: DES.

DEPARTMENT OF EDUCATION AND SCIENCE (1989) *Planning for School Development: Advice to Governors, Headteachers and Teachers.* London: DES.

DEPARTMENT OF EDUCATION AND SCIENCE (1991) *Development Planning: A Practical Guide.* London: DES.

DEPARTMENT FOR EDUCATION (1992) *Choice and Diversity: A New Framework for Schools.* London: HMSO.

DEPARTMENT FOR EDUCATION (1993) *Inspecting Schools: A Guide to the Inspection Provisions of the Education (Schools) Act 1992 in England*, Circular 7/93. London: DFE.

Everard, B. and Morris, G. (1990) *Effective School Management.* London: Paul Chapman Publishing.

Fullan, M. (1991) *The New Meaning of Educational Change.* London: Cassell.

Giles, C. (1995b) 'Site-based Planning and Resource Management: The Role of the School Development Plan'. *Educational Change and Development*, Vol. 15 (2), pp 45-50.

Giles, C. (1995a) 'School-Based Planning: Are UK Schools Grasping the Strategic Initiative?'. *International Journal of Educational Management*, Vol. 9 (4), pp 4-7.

Giles, C. (1995c) 'Marketing, Parental Choice and Strategic Planning: an Opportunity or Dilemma for UK Schools?'

International Journal of Educational Reform, Vol. 4, (1, January), pp 25-28.

Handy, C. B. (1985) *Understanding Organisations*. London: Penguin Books.

Hardie, B. (1991) *Marketing the Primary School*. Plymouth: Northcote House.

Hardie, B. (1995) *Evaluating the Primary School: a Practical Guide to the Evaluation Process*. Plymouth: Northcote House.

Hargreaves, D. H. and Hopkins, D. (1991) *The Empowered School: The Management and Practice of Development Planning*. London: Cassell.

Hargreaves, D. H. (1991) 'Changing School Culture Through Development Planning', in Tiddell, S. and Brown, S. *School Effectiveness Research: Its Messages for School Improvement*. Edinburgh: HMSO.

Hopkins, D. (1989) *Evaluation for School Development*. Milton Keynes: Open University.

HM Inspectors of Schools, Scottish Office Education Department (SOED) (1991). 'The Role of School Development Plans in Managing School Effectiveness', *Management of Educational Resources 5*. Edinburgh: HMI.

OFFICE FOR STANDARDS IN EDUCATION (OFSTED) (1992) *The Handbook for the Inspection of Schools*. London: HMSO.

Skelton, M., Playfoot, D. and Reeves, G. (1991) *Development Planning for Primary Schools*. London: Routledge.

Stoll, L. and Fink, D. (1992) 'Effecting School Change: The Halton Approach', *School Effectiveness and Improvement*, vol. 3(1), pp. 19–41.

Stoner, J. A. F. (1982) *Management*, 2nd edition. London: Prentice Hall.

Index